TABLE OF CONTENT

Chapter 1: Valkyrie Mythology in Norse Lore 1

Origin and etymology of Valkyries 1

Role as divine messengers and attendants of Odin 3

Chapter 2: Valkyries as Choosers of the Slain 7

The concept of Valhalla and its connection to Valkyries 7

The Valkyries' power to select 10

Chapter 3: Valkyries in Nor...

Valkyries in the Poetic Edda

Their appearances, attributes, and ... deities 6

Chapter 4: Folklore and Legends of Valkyries 20

Stories and myths about Valkyries in different cultures 20

Their association with death, prophecy, and warfare 23

Chapter 5: Valkyries in Modern Interpretation 26

Evolution of Valkyrie mythology in modern literature and pop culture 26

Their depiction in popular media and its impact on public perception 28

Chapter 6: Valkyries in Art and Mythology 32

Artistic representations of Valkyries from ancient times to the present 32

Symbolism and significance in different artistic mediums ...35

Chapter 7: Valkyries and Gender 39

The ambiguous gender roles of Valkyries 39

Their portrayal as female warriors and as divine attendants 42

Chapter 8: Valkyries and Destiny 45

The role of Valkyries in shaping human destiny 45

Their connection to the Fates and the cycles of life and death 48

Chapter 9: Valkyries and Supernatural Beings 51

Valkyries' interactions with other supernatural entities in Norse mythology 51

Their relationships with Odin, Thor, and other gods 54

Chapter 10: Valkyries in Ritual and Practice 57

Rituals and practices associated with Valkyries in Norse culture 57

The significance of invoking Valkyries for protection and guidance 59

Chapter 11: Valkyrie Traditions and Customs 63

Cultural customs and traditions surrounding Valkyries 63

Their role in funeral rituals and the afterlife 66

Chapter 12: Valkyries and the Afterlife 69

Valkyries as guides and protectors of the dead 69

Their influence on the realms of Valhalla and Hel................72

Chapter 1: Valkyrie Mythology in Norse Lore

Origin and etymology of Valkyries

Delving into the origins and etymology of the Valkyries necessitates a nuanced understanding of Old Norse language and the cultural context within which these figures emerged. The very term "Valkyrie" itself is a compound word, revealing much about their role and perceived nature. It derives from the Old Norse valkyrja, composed of valr meaning "slain warriors" or "the host of the slain," and kyrja, which translates to "chooser" or "selector." This simple linguistic breakdown immediately establishes a core function: the Valkyries are the choosers of the fallen. The etymology speaks not just to their activity but their agency; they are not passive observers of battle, but active participants in determining the fate of those who perish in conflict.

The absence of a singular, definitive origin myth for the Valkyries points to their gradual evolution within Norse mythology rather than a sudden, fully-formed creation. They weren't born from a single divine act but appear to have developed from a complex interplay of evolving societal values, religious beliefs, and poetic imagery. Their roles seem to have expanded and shifted over time, reflecting changes in Viking society and their worldview. The initial concept of a female figure associated with death and battle likely predates the fully articulated Valkyrie figure we know from later sagas and Eddas. It's plausible that early iterations of these figures were less clearly defined, possibly incorporating elements of other supernatural beings, or existing as more generalized embodiments of fate and battlefield destiny.

The development of the Valkyrie concept is inextricably linked to the evolving understanding of death and honor in Norse culture. The intense focus on glory in battle and the afterlife in Valhalla likely played a significant role in shaping the Valkyrie's image. The concept of a warrior's death in battle as an honorable path to a glorious afterlife, a journey overseen by powerful female figures, served to reinforce both the societal value of martial prowess and the belief in a structured, divinely-ordered afterlife. Thus, the etymology of the Valkyries' name, emphasizing their role in choosing the fallen, reflects a deeply ingrained cultural fascination with death in battle, viewed not as an end but a transition to another realm of existence.

The poetic and literary evidence from the Old Norse texts offers further insights into the gradual evolution of the Valkyrie archetype. Their depictions shift in different sources, suggesting a fluid and evolving understanding rather than a fixed, immutable definition. In some texts, they are presented as independent agents of fate, empowered to make life-or-death decisions; in others, they function as messengers or servants of Odin, receiving explicit orders. This discrepancy suggests the image of the Valkyrie was not a monolithic creation, but rather a concept refined and reshaped over time, adapting to the narrative needs and evolving interpretations of their role in the Norse cosmos. The evolving narratives, in themselves, contribute to the richness of their etymology, reflecting not a single, fixed origin, but a process of continuous redefinition.

Furthermore, the linguistic connections between valkyrja and similar terms within Germanic languages illuminate the broader cultural context. Comparative linguistics allows us to trace the evolution of concepts related to female figures associated with death and fate across different Germanic cultures. While variations exist in their names and specific functions, the common threads suggest a shared Proto-Germanic root for these figures, indicating a deep-seated, pre-Viking understanding of female figures possessing power over life and death, specifically in the context of battle and the afterlife. This broader comparative analysis significantly enriches our understanding of the valkyrja etymology, revealing its place within a broader tapestry of Germanic myth and folklore. The Valkyrie, then, is not simply a product of Old Norse culture, but a figure reflecting the shared history and beliefs of a larger Germanic cultural sphere. The etymological exploration thus provides a pathway to understanding the historical and cultural layers that shaped the image and role of the Valkyries. The very name itself – a carefully crafted compound word – encapsulates a rich and evolving tradition.

Role as divine messengers and attendants of Odin

The Valkyries, in the tapestry of Norse mythology, are far more than mere battlefield gleaners, selecting the worthy slain to populate Odin's hall, Valhalla. Their role as divine messengers and attendants of the Allfather extends far beyond this commonly understood function, weaving a complex and multifaceted narrative that reveals their profound importance within the broader cosmological framework. They are not simply passive agents of Odin's will, but active participants in the divine drama, embodying the potent intersection of war, fate, and the very fabric of existence itself. Their agency extends to the transmission of vital information, prophecies, and divine pronouncements, establishing a crucial link between the mortal realm and the celestial sphere governed by Odin. Their flights across the battlefields are not merely a spectacle of ethereal beauty; they represent the ceaseless flow of information, the constant communication between the realms of gods and men, a communication essential for maintaining cosmic balance and order.

This communicative function transcends mere reporting on the progress of wars. The Valkyries are portrayed as possessing an intimate understanding of the intricate workings of fate, wielding a knowledge of both the past and the future, able to decipher the hidden currents of destiny. Their pronouncements, often cryptic and laden with symbolic language, are not merely observations but active participations in shaping events. They act as conduits of Odin's prophetic pronouncements, whispering secrets into the ears of kings and heroes, influencing the course of battles and even the destinies of entire nations. This ability to both report and influence underlines their significance as far more than simple messengers; they are active players in the unfolding narrative of the cosmos, acting as both observers and participants in the intricate dance of fate. Their knowledge is not passively received; it is actively sought and strategically deployed, suggesting a level of intelligence and cunning that surpasses their often-romanticized image as mere beautiful warriors.

The Valkyrie's attendance upon Odin extends beyond the battlefield and the realms of prophecy. Their presence in his hall, Valhalla, speaks to their role as both servants and advisors. While they serve him by ensuring a steady supply of warriors for the upcoming Ragnarok, their intimate proximity suggests a far deeper connection. They are not simply waitresses serving mead; they are privy to the Allfather's innermost counsels, participants in his most profound deliberations. Their privileged position grants them access to information unavailable to other gods or mortals, suggesting that their role extends to strategic planning, military advice, and even the formulation of divine policies affecting the mortal realm. This intimate participation in Odin's court underscores their profound importance within the divine hierarchy, establishing them as more than mere messengers, but key players in the administration of Asgard and the governance of the cosmos.

This elevated status is further underscored by their often-ambiguous relationship with mortality. While they are divine beings, inhabiting the realm of the gods, their connection to the mortal world is profoundly strong. Their ability to traverse the boundaries between realms, between life and death, between the divine and the mortal, speaks to their unique position within the cosmological order. They are not simply messengers between two separate entities, but bridges, connectors, embodiments of the fluidity and interconnectedness that define the Norse worldview. This unique ability to interact with both the living and the dead reinforces their function as mediators, as interpreters, as agents of change and transformation, acting as the living embodiment of the permeable membrane between the realms.

Moreover, the individual Valkyries are often depicted with unique attributes, reflecting their diverse functions and abilities. Some are known for their prowess in battle, others for their wisdom and prophetic insights, while others still are characterized by their beauty and charm. This diversity reflects the multifaceted nature of their role, emphasizing that they are not a homogenous group, but rather a collection of individuals, each contributing their unique skills and talents to the overall function of the divine court. This internal diversity underlines the complex nature of their relationship with Odin, and the wide-ranging responsibilities they shoulder. They are not a singular entity, but a constellation of individuals with diverse capacities, collectively serving the multifaceted needs of the Allfather.

The visual imagery associated with the Valkyries – their winged steeds, their shining armor, their ethereal beauty – further underscores their role as messengers of the divine. Their swift flight across the heavens, their ability to traverse vast distances in a blink of an eye, represent the speed and efficiency of divine communication. Their appearance, both awe-inspiring and terrifying, reflects the power and authority inherent in their messages. Their iconic imagery serves not merely as a visual representation, but as an active component of their function, a visual reinforcement of their authority and the importance of the messages they carry. The aesthetics of their depiction serve as a potent symbol of the divine power they represent, embodying the awe-inspiring might of Odin and his celestial court.

Finally, the enduring presence of the Valkyries in Norse mythology and their subsequent influence on literature, art, and popular culture testify to the depth and complexity of their role. Their continued relevance underscores the enduring power of their symbolic representation, their status as powerful agents within the divine scheme, and the profound importance of their function as messengers and attendants of the Allfather. Their enduring appeal lies not only in their captivating visual imagery, but also in their embodiment of several key aspects of the Norse cosmology: the interconnectedness of realms, the fluid nature of fate, and the powerful dynamic between the divine and the mortal.

Their complex and multifaceted roles ensure that their legacy continues to resonate, inspiring awe and fascination centuries after the fall of the Norse pantheon. They are more than simply messengers; they are living embodiments of the divine will, the celestial agents who actively shape the destiny of mortals and gods alike, a testament to their enduring significance in the rich tapestry of Norse mythology.

.

Chapter 2: Valkyries as Choosers of the Slain

The concept of Valhalla and its connection to Valkyries

Valhalla, the majestic hall of the slain in Norse mythology, exists in inextricable symbiosis with the Valkyries, its celestial gatekeepers and selective inhabitants. The very concept of Valhalla, a glittering palace in Asgard ruled by the god Odin, hinges entirely on the Valkyries' agency. It is not merely a grand hall; it's a meticulously curated assembly of the most valiant warriors, chosen specifically by these divine maidens of war. This selective process, far from being arbitrary, underscores the profound connection between the warrior ethos, the divine realm, and the afterlife promised to those deemed worthy by the Valkyries. The hall's grandeur, its endless feasts and glorious battles, are all reflections of the warriors' prowess, a testament to the Valkyries' discerning judgment. Without the Valkyries, Valhalla remains a hollow shell, an empty promise; it is their tireless selection process that imbues the hall with its legendary significance and its perpetual, vibrant life. The Valkyries are not simply messengers or servants; they are the architects of Valhalla's composition, actively shaping its essence and reflecting the values of the Norse warrior ideal. Their choices directly define who enters this prestigious afterlife, forging a link between earthly heroism and divine recognition.

The connection isn't merely functional; it's deeply symbolic. The Valkyries, often depicted as riding swift steeds across the battlefields, represent the very forces of fate and destiny, selecting those who embody the qualities Odin seeks in his warrior elite. This selective process elevates Valhalla beyond a simple reward for a good death; it becomes a reflection of divine judgment, a validation of the warrior's earthly life and actions. The Valkyries' role, therefore, transforms Valhalla from a mere location into a potent symbol of honour, courage, and the ultimate test of a warrior's mettle. It's not enough to die bravely; one must be chosen to gain access to Valhalla's glory. This bestows upon the Valkyries a power that transcends mere mortal perception; they are the arbiters of heroic destiny, determining who attains the ultimate accolade of entry into Odin's legendary hall. The warrior's yearning for Valhalla, then, is intrinsically linked to the possibility of recognition by the Valkyries, reinforcing their pivotal role in shaping the afterlife's meaning and its prestige.

The inherent selectivity of the Valkyries' actions also throws into sharp relief the values underpinning the Norse worldview. Valhalla is not a democracy of the dead; it is an elite assembly reserved for those who demonstrate exceptional courage, skill, and loyalty in battle. This selective process, orchestrated by the Valkyries, highlights the high regard the Norse held for martial prowess and the importance of individual achievement within a warrior culture. The Valkyries, acting as divine judges, uphold and enforce these ideals, ensuring that only the most worthy warriors grace the halls of Valhalla. This reinforces the idea that death in battle, while a significant event, is not the sole criterion for entrance; rather, it's the quality of that death, the actions and character that precede it, which determines whether the Valkyrie's spear will point towards Valhalla or a different, less glorious fate. The rigorous selection process emphasizes the Norse reverence for a warrior's honour and their unwavering dedication to the glory of their clan and gods.

Moreover, the relationship between the Valkyries and Valhalla underscores the interconnectedness between the mortal and divine realms in Norse cosmology. The Valkyries, as divine beings, act as the conduit between the earthly battlefield and the celestial afterlife. They are not merely witnesses to the clash of steel; they actively participate in shaping its outcome by selecting those who will be transported to Valhalla. This constant interaction between earthly actions and divine judgment vividly illustrates the belief system's inherent dynamism and the tangible consequences of one's actions. The Valkyries' presence on the battlefield, their intervention in the flow of battle, blurs the lines between the mortal and divine spheres, illustrating a universe where the gods are not passive observers but active participants in the shaping of human destiny. This constant interplay highlights the belief that heroic deeds performed on earth have direct and significant consequences in the afterlife, a system of cosmic reciprocity underpinned by the Valkyries' unwavering selection process.

Further analysis reveals the symbolic significance of the Valkyries' physical characteristics and actions. Their often-depicted appearance – winged maidens adorned with armour and weaponry – speaks to the merging of feminine grace and martial power. Their flight across the battlefields represents the swiftness and impartiality of fate, their spears selecting victims not based on personal preference but on an assessment of their valor. The imagery of the Valkyries collecting the slain, carefully choosing which souls to carry to Valhalla, also speaks to a deliberate and considered afterlife, not a random or haphazard transition from life to death. The meticulous nature of this process, far from being arbitrary, speaks to a deeply structured and purposeful cosmos, one in which even death is not devoid of meaning or divine agency. The Valkyrie's role, therefore, elevates the concept of death itself, transforming it from a simple ending into a vital component of a divinely ordained cosmic order, a transition carefully orchestrated and ultimately judged by these celestial figures.

Finally, the mythology surrounding Valhalla and the Valkyries provides a profound insight into the Norse worldview regarding heroism and the afterlife. It highlights the importance of bravery, loyalty, and skill in battle, qualities that were paramount in Norse society. Valhalla, as a reward for these attributes, becomes not just a place, but a powerful symbol of the ultimate achievement within that culture. This is inextricably linked to the Valkyries, who are not just impartial judges, but active participants in the shaping of this ultimate reward. Their actions reinforce the values of their society and highlight the strong link between the mortal and divine worlds. The narrative of Valhalla and the Valkyries, therefore, transcends a mere recounting of mythical events; it serves as a powerful encapsulation of Norse cultural values, aspirations, and beliefs about the afterlife, all carefully woven together by the role of the Valkyries as the ultimate choosers of the slain. The very existence of Valhalla, its glory and its occupants, are wholly dependent on the Valkyries' unwavering dedication to their celestial duty, thus rendering them crucial figures in understanding the heart of Norse mythology.

.

The Valkyries' power to select warriors for afterlife

The Valkyries' power to select warriors for the afterlife transcends a simple function; it represents a complex interplay of divine agency, martial prowess, and the very fabric of Norse cosmology. Their role isn't merely that of passive observers choosing from a battlefield's carnage, but rather active participants shaping the composition of Odin's hall, Valhalla. This selectivity isn't arbitrary; it speaks volumes about the values of the Norse worldview and the criteria by which heroic merit was assessed. The Valkyries, as choosers, weren't simply identifying the physically strongest or most prolific killers. Their judgment extended beyond brute force to encompass a nuanced understanding of courage, honor, and adherence to the warrior ethos. A warrior's death, therefore, wasn't the sole determinant of their eligibility for Valhalla; the manner of their death, the context of their battle, and the quality of their fighting spirit were all crucial factors influencing the Valkyries' decisions. This selective process elevated the afterlife beyond a mere reward for mortality; it transformed it into a meritocratic realm populated by those deemed worthy by divine arbiters, solidifying the status of Valhalla as a symbol of exceptional heroism. The very act of selection imbued the afterlife with an aura of prestige, heightening its desirability and reinforcing the warrior culture's ideals.

The agency wielded by the Valkyries is further underscored by the nature of their appearance and their symbolic associations. They are depicted as powerful, often ethereal beings, riding their steeds across battlefields, cloaked in the mists of war and death. This imagery isn't accidental; it reinforces their supernatural authority and their ability to transcend the mundane constraints of the earthly realm. Their association with Odin, the Allfather himself, solidifies their status as divine agents, underscoring the sanctity and importance of their task. They are not merely messengers or servants; they are active participants in the cosmic drama of life and death, wielding a power that directly shapes the composition of the afterlife. This active role positions them not as passive recorders of events, but as influencers of destiny, directly impacting the fate of those who fall in battle. The very act of being chosen by a Valkyrie elevates a warrior's status beyond mere mortality, transforming them into a member of an exclusive, elite company – the chosen warriors of Odin, forever enshrined in the annals of Norse mythology.

The power of selection goes beyond the individual warrior; it also impacts the larger societal structure. By choosing those deemed worthy, the Valkyries indirectly reinforced the social hierarchy and the values of Norse society. Their choices acted as a powerful form of social commentary, highlighting the ideals the culture prized. It wasn't simply about strength; it was about honor, bravery, and adherence to the warrior code. The Valkyries' choices, therefore, played a crucial role in shaping social norms and perpetuating a warrior ethos that valued honor, courage, and a willingness to face death in battle. The selective process contributed to the creation and maintenance of a culture that celebrated heroism and martial excellence, fostering a societal structure where the pursuit of glory on the battlefield was not only accepted but actively encouraged. This inherent power dynamic, where the divine actively influences the mortal realm by shaping the composition of the afterlife, created a powerful feedback loop that reinforced the very values of Norse society.

Furthermore, the ambiguity surrounding the Valkyries' criteria for selection adds another layer of complexity. While tales generally point toward valor and martial prowess as key factors, the absence of a rigidly defined set of rules allows for a degree of interpretive freedom. This ambiguity hints at a more nuanced understanding of heroism that extends beyond simple metrics. The subjective nature of the Valkyries' judgment reflects the inherent complexities of human experience and the difficulty of objectively measuring heroic deeds. This ambiguity also allows for the possibility of divine favoritism or the influence of other factors beyond mortal understanding. The lack of a clear-cut formula reinforces the sense of awe and mystery surrounding the Valkyries and their power, further cementing their position as powerful, enigmatic figures within the Norse pantheon. The very act of selection becomes shrouded in a sense of divine judgment, leaving mortals uncertain about the exact criteria that determine eligibility for Valhalla, adding to the legend's mystique and power.

The Valkyries' power, therefore, isn't confined to the simple act of choosing warriors for Valhalla. It encompasses a much broader influence, shaping the Norse worldview, reinforcing societal values, and acting as a powerful symbol of divine agency. Their choices were not merely administrative tasks but active participations in the cosmic order, subtly shaping the dynamics of both the earthly and the otherworldly realms. The selectivity inherent in their role elevated the afterlife to a realm of meritocracy, rewarding valor and reinforcing the cultural values central to Norse society. The stories of the Valkyries, far from being simple tales of afterlife selection, serve as intricate commentaries on the nature of heroism, the complexities of divine justice, and the enduring power of cultural ideals, ensuring their place as enduring figures in Norse mythology and its ongoing interpretation. The power of choice they possessed is not simply a function, but a powerful force which shapes the very narrative of Norse cosmology, influencing the living and the dead alike. Their ability to select transcends simple mortality; it is a cosmic act of judgment and creation, simultaneously defining the afterlife and reflecting the values of the earthly realm. The Valkyries, in their capacity as choosers of the slain, are far more than mere messengers; they are active agents of destiny, shaping the very fabric of the Norse universe.

Chapter 3: Valkyries in Norse Literature

Valkyries in the Poetic Edda and Prose Edda

Valkyries, the "choosers of the slain," occupy a fascinating and multifaceted role within the complex tapestry of Norse mythology, as depicted in both the Poetic Edda and the Prose Edda. Their portrayal transcends simple battlefield attendants; they are powerful figures intertwined with fate, war, and the divine, possessing agency and influence that ripple through the narrative fabric of these foundational texts. A nuanced analysis reveals their diverse functions and symbolic weight, moving beyond simplistic interpretations to illuminate the subtle intricacies of their characterization.

The Poetic Edda, a collection of poems reflecting diverse oral traditions, presents Valkyries in dynamic and sometimes contradictory ways. Their involvement in battles is consistently emphasized, yet their roles extend far beyond mere battlefield observers. Poems such as the "Völuspá" allude to their participation in the creation of the cosmos, suggesting a connection to primordial forces that predates even the conflict between gods and giants. This hints at a deeper significance, positioning them not just as agents of death but as intrinsic elements within the cosmic order itself. Their power is subtly showcased in their ability to influence the outcome of battles; they are not merely recorders of fate, but shapers of it, choosing which warriors will fall and which will prevail. This manipulation of destiny aligns them with the broader themes of fate and free will so prevalent in Norse cosmology, suggesting a complex interaction between preordained events and the agency of these powerful female figures. The evocative imagery employed in these poems reinforces their otherworldly nature, painting them as ethereal beings who glide through the air, their movements imbued with a supernatural grace that underscores their connection to the divine realm. This is further enhanced by their association with Odin, the Allfather, suggesting a direct link to the highest echelons of power within the Norse pantheon. The warrior-like attributes attributed to them in certain poems – their prowess in battle, their ability to wield weapons – challenges the typical gender roles of the era, presenting them as formidable figures who command respect, not merely through their association with the gods, but through their own inherent strength and power.

The Prose Edda, compiled centuries later by Snorri Sturluson, offers a more systematic, albeit arguably less nuanced, perspective on Valkyries. Here, they are more explicitly presented as servants of Odin, tasked with collecting the souls of fallen heroes to populate Valhalla, his heavenly hall. This interpretation emphasizes their role as intermediaries between the mortal and divine realms, guiding the worthy warriors to their afterlife reward. However, the Prose Edda doesn't diminish their inherent power; instead, it frames it within a more structured context of Odin's overarching authority. This portrayal reveals a shift in perspective, potentially reflecting evolving societal views on gender and power. The meticulous descriptions of their appearance, their weaponry, and their attire in the Prose Edda, despite their function as messengers of death, suggests a lingering fascination with their formidable stature and mystical allure. This emphasis on their physical attributes complements their otherworldly nature, reinforcing the notion of them as beings simultaneously ethereal and powerfully physical, reflecting the ambiguous nature of death and the afterlife within Norse mythology.

The contrasts and convergences between the depictions of Valkyries in the Poetic and Prose Eddas offer a rich ground for analysis. While the Poetic Edda emphasizes their involvement in shaping the broader cosmological events and their intrinsic connection to fate, the Prose Edda presents a more structured portrayal, emphasizing their role as Odin's attendants. However, both versions underscore the Valkyries' inherent power and their significance as crucial figures within the Norse mythological framework. The inconsistencies may reflect the evolution of oral traditions over time or differing interpretations of the same figures, showcasing the dynamism of Norse mythology and its capacity for multiple perspectives. Regardless of the specific context, the Valkyries emerge as potent symbols, embodying both the harsh realities of war and the mystical allure of the afterlife, their significance extending far beyond their function as mere battlefield attendants. Their agency in choosing the slain, their connection to the gods, and their supernatural abilities cement their position as some of the most compelling and enigmatic figures in Norse mythology. The enduring fascination with these powerful women continues to resonate today, a testament to the depth and complexity of their portrayal in the Eddas and their lasting impact on our understanding of Norse cosmology and its multifaceted worldview. The shifting perspectives across the two Eddas enrich the understanding of their roles, showcasing their evolving interpretations within a dynamic mythological landscape that resists simplistic categorization and rewards deeper exploration of their varied functions and symbolic weight.

.

Their appearances, attributes, and relationships with other deities

The Valkyries, those enigmatic figures of Norse mythology, hold a position of unique power and allure, their appearances, attributes, and relationships with other deities woven intricately into the very fabric of the cosmos. Their visual representation, while not uniformly depicted across all surviving sources, consistently evokes a sense of ethereal beauty combined with formidable strength. Frequently portrayed as young women, often adorned in shining armor, their clothing and weaponry reflect both their celestial origins and their martial roles. Descriptions often highlight shimmering garments, perhaps woven from starlight or the aurora borealis, alongside weaponry imbued with otherworldly power. Their mounts, frequently described as steeds with the breath of fire or wings of the wind, mirror their own exceptional capabilities, further emphasizing their divine connection and fierce independence. These attributes—the luminous clothing, the celestial weaponry, the magnificent steeds—all serve to underscore their position as intermediaries between the mortal and divine realms, beings both breathtakingly beautiful and terrifyingly powerful in their celestial authority.

This dual nature, the striking juxtaposition of beauty and lethal capability, permeates the very essence of the Valkyries. They are not simply passive observers of battle; they actively participate in its unfolding, selecting the fallen warriors destined for Valhalla, Odin's hall of the slain. This power of choice, this ability to determine the ultimate fate of mortal heroes, places them in a position of immense influence, a divine authority that even other deities might envy. Their selective judgment, far from arbitrary, reflects a discerning assessment of warrior prowess, courage, and loyalty. Their very act of choosing, therefore, elevates the slain to a higher plane of existence, bestowing upon them a form of immortality and a place within the glorious company of Odin's chosen warriors. This selective power is not merely a function of their proximity to Odin; it reflects an inherent capacity for judgment, a divine wisdom that transcends mere obedience.

The Valkyries' relationship with Odin forms the cornerstone of their divine identity. They are, in many accounts, explicitly described as his handmaidens, messengers, and servants. However, this relationship is far from one of simple subservience. While they undoubtedly carry out Odin's will, they possess a considerable degree of autonomy and agency. Their independent action in the heat of battle, their selective choices among the fallen, all suggest a level of authority that surpasses that of a mere attendant. This dynamic interplay between subservience and independence, between obedience and agency, contributes significantly to their complex and fascinating character. Furthermore, their connection to other deities, while less prominently featured in surviving texts, suggests broader interactions within the Norse pantheon. Their presence on the battlefields, their participation in feasts and gatherings of the gods, points towards a role within the broader divine society, one that transcends their specific connection to Odin. Their influence extends beyond the halls of Valhalla, subtly shaping the destiny of both gods and mortals alike.

The inherent ambiguity surrounding their specific roles and functions only adds to their mysterious allure. While often associated with death and warfare, their connection to fate, prophecy, and the weaving of destinies suggests a deeper involvement in the very fabric of existence. They are not simply agents of death; they are shapers of destiny, their choices influencing the course of wars and the fate of entire lineages. This nuanced role, this multifaceted portrayal, defies simplistic categorization, making them endlessly captivating figures within Norse mythology. Their connections to other deities, while less extensively detailed, hint at further layers of interaction within the Norse cosmological framework. Their presence at feasts, their participation in divine gatherings, all suggest a complex web of relationships that extends beyond their primary allegiance to Odin. The sparse details offer fertile ground for interpretation and speculation, enriching the mythological narrative and adding to the enduring fascination of these ethereal warriors.

The imagery surrounding the Valkyries often features symbolic motifs that reinforce their connection to both the living and the dead. Birds, particularly ravens and swans, are frequently associated with them, reflecting their swiftness, their ability to traverse vast distances between the realms, and their connection to the messages of the gods. These avian associations not only highlight their swiftness and their connection to divine communication, but also emphasize their ability to move effortlessly between the mortal and divine realms, embodying a fluidity of movement that mirrors their ability to shape destiny. The very act of choosing the slain, the selection of those deemed worthy of Valhalla, underscores their power to determine the ultimate fate of warriors. This power, this ability to influence the afterlife, sets them apart from other divine figures, placing them in a unique position of influence and authority within the cosmos. Their connection to fate, their involvement in the weaving of destinies, further underscores their profound importance within the overall Norse cosmological scheme. Their visual portrayal, their attributes, and their relationships with other deities, all combine to create a compelling and enduring image of these powerful, enigmatic figures who choose the slain. The lack of extensive detail regarding their interactions with other gods only serves to enhance their mystery, leaving room for scholarly debate and creative interpretation, ultimately ensuring the enduring fascination with these figures of Norse mythology. The Valkyries, in their enigmatic and powerful roles, remain captivating figures of Norse mythology, their impact resonating across centuries of storytelling and scholarly interpretation.

.

Chapter 4: Folklore and Legends of Valkyries

Stories and myths about Valkyries in different cultures

The tapestry of Valkyrie lore, woven across centuries and diverse cultures, reveals a fascinating evolution of these powerful figures. While their most prominent association lies within the Norse pantheon, the echoes of their archetype resonate in other mythologies, albeit often subtly transformed. The core concept – the choosing and guiding of the fallen – remains a consistent thread, but the specifics of their roles, their appearance, and even their ultimate fate vary wildly depending on the cultural lens through which they are viewed. Examining these variations illuminates not only the rich tapestry of mythology itself but also the anxieties and aspirations of the cultures that birthed these compelling figures.

The Norse Valkyries, famously depicted as ethereal warriors riding winged steeds, are the most deeply explored and widely known. Their selection process, often depicted as a battlefield spectacle, reveals a complex interplay of fate and merit. Not all slain warriors are deemed worthy; the Valkyries choose those who displayed exceptional courage, skill, and adherence to a warrior's code. This selective process underscores the Norse societal emphasis on honor and martial prowess. Beyond their battlefield duties, the Valkyries serve as attendants to Odin, preparing feasts in Valhalla, the hall of the slain heroes, highlighting their role as intermediaries between the mortal and divine realms. The stories surrounding them often portray their beauty and power intertwined, suggesting that these figures represent not just death, but also a form of transcendent glory. Their individual names, like Brunhilde and Brynhildr, frequently appear in sagas and eddas, often at the center of complex narratives involving love, betrayal, and the tragic consequences of defying the gods' decrees. The ambiguity surrounding their ultimate nature – divine beings, powerful spirits, or even magically enhanced mortal women – adds another layer of complexity to their already multifaceted representation.

Contrasting the clear-cut image of the Norse Valkyrie, the echoes of similar figures in other cultures present a more nuanced picture. In Celtic mythology, while no direct equivalent exists, the concept of powerful female figures guiding souls to the afterlife can be found within the broader context of their beliefs. The presence of female deities associated with death and the underworld, although not explicitly warrior-like in their depiction, hints at a potential influence or parallel. Their roles, while not directly involved in the battlefield selection, nonetheless fulfill a similar function of mediating the transition from the mortal realm to the afterlife. The inherent power and often ambivalent nature of these goddesses, possessing both life-giving and death-dealing capacities, suggests a thematic resonance with the Valkyries' capacity for both destruction and selection. The lack of explicit narrative details prevents direct comparison, but the underlying archetype suggests a shared cultural understanding of the significance of female figures within the realm of death and fate.

Moving further afield, aspects of the Valkyrie archetype can be discerned in various indigenous belief systems, although the narrative threads are often less explicitly defined. Many cultures feature figures who act as psychopomps, guiding the souls of the dead to the afterlife. These individuals, while not always depicted as warriors, share the key characteristic of mediating between life and death, a crucial component of the Valkyrie's function. The specifics of their actions, their appearance, and their relationship to the divine vary greatly, reflecting the unique cosmologies of different cultures. These differences, however, do not necessarily negate the possibility of a shared, archetypal origin. The consistent recurrence of female figures within this role suggests a universally recognized element of female power associated with death and transition. The symbolic weight given to these figures, often depicted with extraordinary abilities or close ties to the spiritual world, points toward a universal fascination with the agency and authority exerted by females within the realm of mortality and beyond.

The variations in the portrayal of these Valkyrie-like figures across different cultures highlight the diverse ways societies conceptualize death, heroism, and the afterlife. The specific details differ drastically, but the underlying theme of powerful female figures guiding the passage to the afterlife reveals a remarkable degree of cross-cultural resonance. While the image of the winged warrior remains strongly linked to the Norse mythology, the presence of similar archetypes in different cultures serves as a powerful reminder of the universal human fascination with death, the journey beyond, and the role of powerful female figures in shaping that journey. The evolution of the Valkyrie myth, from the vividly described Norse warriors to the more subtle echoes in other cultures, is a testament to the enduring power of archetypes and the persistent human need to understand and grapple with the mysteries surrounding life and death. The cultural variations emphasize the malleability of myth, its capacity to adapt and reflect the unique concerns and aspirations of different communities, while the underlying similarities speak to the universal themes that underpin these narratives. The Valkyrie, therefore, serves not only as a fascinating figure of Norse mythology but also as a compelling example of the ways in which shared human experiences are expressed and transformed through diverse cultural lenses. The enduring presence of this figure, in myriad forms across cultures, indicates a deeply rooted fascination with the concept of female agency in the face of mortality, the power of choice, and the enduring mystery of what lies beyond.

.

Their association with death, prophecy, and warfare

The Valkyries, those ethereal figures of Norse mythology, are inextricably linked to the brutal realities of death, the veiled uncertainties of prophecy, and the chaotic fury of warfare. Their association with these three domains isn't simply coincidental; it forms the very core of their being, weaving a complex tapestry of power, fate, and the ever-present shadow of mortality. They are not mere bystanders to the violent ebb and flow of battle, but active participants, their choices shaping the destinies of both the living and the dead. Their power to choose, often described as a selective reaping of souls, highlights the Norse understanding of death not as an end, but as a transition, a journey guided by these divine intermediaries. This selective process further implies an element of judgment, hinting at a cosmic balance maintained by the Valkyries' discerning choices. The warriors who earn their favor are those who have proven their worth in battle, embodying the very ideals of courage, skill, and unwavering ferocity that the Norse culture so revered.

The prophetic element inherent in the Valkyries' actions elevates their role beyond mere battlefield attendants. Their selection isn't arbitrary; it's a reflection of a pre-determined fate, a cosmic script unfolding across the bloody battlefields of Midgard. Their very flights, often depicted as swirling, chaotic dances across the skies, can be interpreted as a reflection of the unpredictable nature of war and fate itself. These flights are not simply aesthetic; they are symbolic representations of the weaving of destiny, each warrior's fate predetermined even as they engage in the brutal dance of conflict. Furthermore, their presence on the battlefield serves as an omen, a harbinger of victory or defeat, their choices foreshadowing the ultimate outcome of the clash of arms. This prophetic function adds another layer of complexity to their character; they are not only arbiters of death but also oracles, their actions echoing the unseen forces that shape the course of human history. Their appearance, whether amidst the storm of battle or perched atop a battlefield hill, speaks to an impending shift in fortune, a change in the cosmic balance meticulously tracked and overseen by these divine agents.

The intimate connection between the Valkyries and warfare goes beyond simply choosing the slain; it's a symbiotic relationship rooted in the very essence of Norse cosmology. They are not passive observers but active participants in the violence, shaping its course and influencing its outcome. Their presence on the battlefield is a tangible manifestation of the divine forces at play, a reminder that the struggles of mortals are subject to the whims of a higher power. Their role is far from neutral; their actions are integral to the unfolding events, their choices influencing the tide of battle. The blood-soaked fields become their hunting grounds, where they choose their prey from amongst the fallen, ensuring that the worthy find their place in the grand afterlife, reinforcing the deeply ingrained Norse warrior ethos. The Valkyries are not merely associated with war; they are woven into its very fabric, shaping its destiny as much as they are shaped by its brutal realities. They represent the divine hand guiding the chaotic dance of conflict, ensuring that only the most worthy find their place in the halls of Valhalla, a testament to their powerful connection to the very concept of heroic death and the ever-present tension between fate and free will. Their imagery, imbued with the power of both death and prophecy, underscores the inherent risks and rewards of the warrior's life, a life intimately intertwined with the Valkyries' choices.

The interwoven nature of death, prophecy, and warfare in the Valkyries' roles extends beyond the battlefield to the broader understanding of Norse cosmology. Their choices, imbued with both judgment and prescience, reflect the cyclical nature of life and death, the constant interplay of fate and free will within the Norse worldview. The selection of the slain is not merely an act of choosing warriors for Valhalla; it's a crucial part of maintaining the cosmic balance, ensuring the continuation of the cycle of existence. This balance, constantly threatened by the chaos of war, is upheld by these divine agents, who are both witnesses and participants in the grand design. Their association with death isn't one of simple grim reaping; it's an active shaping of destiny, a confirmation of the warrior's path and a reflection of the broader cosmic order. The prophetic nature of their actions reveals a world governed by both chance and predetermined fate, a complex tapestry of free will and inevitable destiny intricately woven together. The Valkyries' connection to warfare isn't solely about choosing the dead; it's about influencing the living, encouraging valor and sacrifice in the face of certain mortality, shaping the heroic ideals that formed the very core of Norse society. Their presence on the battlefield, their choices, their very being, is a profound reflection on the Norse understanding of war, death, and the ever-present weight of destiny. The constant interplay between these three elements in the narrative of the Valkyries highlights the richness and complexity of Norse mythology, providing a captivating portrayal of power, fate, and the ever-present dance between life and death.

.

Chapter 5: Valkyries in Modern Interpretation

Evolution of Valkyrie mythology in modern literature and pop culture

The evolution of Valkyrie mythology in modern literature and pop culture reveals a fascinating trajectory, shifting from their initial depiction as fearsome choosers of the slain to complex, multifaceted characters who defy simple categorization. Early 20th-century portrayals often leaned into the traditional imagery: ethereal beings, clad in shining armor, riding winged steeds, and wielding spears, selecting warriors for Odin's hall. This depiction, while respectful of the source material, often lacked depth, presenting them as almost passive agents of fate, their agency limited to their selection process.

However, the latter half of the 20th century and the subsequent rise of feminist thought significantly impacted the portrayal of Valkyries. Authors and artists began to explore the inherent contradictions within the traditional narrative. The power they wielded, choosing the worthy from the battlefield, was inherently a form of judgment, suggesting a degree of independent thought and moral compass often overlooked in earlier interpretations. This led to a reimagining of Valkyries as potent female figures, not simply messengers of death, but agents of destiny, wielding their power with a complex blend of compassion and ruthless efficiency. Their roles ceased to be solely defined by their association with male-dominated warfare, evolving to encompass broader themes of fate, justice, and the cyclical nature of life and death.

This feminist reinterpretation isn't solely confined to literature. The influence is equally evident in video games, where Valkyries often appear as powerful warrior-women, capable of independent action and commanding respect. Their design often reflects this updated perspective, moving beyond the stereotypical "damsel in distress" trope towards representations of fierce independence and unmatched martial prowess. The visual language employed – armor designs, weaponry, and overall aesthetic – reflects a departure from passive representations to active participation in shaping narrative arcs. They are no longer mere supporting characters; they become pivotal figures driving plot and influencing outcomes.

The impact of fantasy literature and role-playing games is undeniable in shaping modern Valkyrie portrayals. The inherent flexibility of the source material allowed for creative expansion, enabling authors and game designers to explore diverse aspects of the Valkyries' personalities and motivations. Their relationships with both gods and mortals become more nuanced, moving beyond simple adherence to divine commands. This newfound complexity allows for the exploration of internal conflicts, moral dilemmas, and emotional depth, adding layers of humanity to these initially ethereal figures. Love, loss, betrayal, and even rebellion against their appointed roles are now common themes.

Furthermore, the rise of "strong female characters" in popular media has undeniably influenced the portrayal of Valkyries. They are often depicted as skilled strategists, powerful combatants, and charismatic leaders, shattering traditional representations of passive female archetypes. This active participation in shaping their own destinies contributes to their evolving persona, showcasing not simply obedience to a higher power, but a proactive agency that defines their character. The ambiguity inherent in the original mythology allows for a range of interpretations, enabling these adaptations to address contemporary issues of power, gender, and morality.

The appropriation of Valkyrie imagery in heavy metal music and other art forms further contributes to the ongoing evolution of their mythology. The powerful imagery of winged warriors resonates powerfully with the genre's themes of rebellion, power, and the struggle against overwhelming forces. These artistic interpretations often amplify the aspects of fierce independence and uncompromising strength, further cementing the Valkyrie's image as an icon of powerful womanhood. This diverse range of visual and auditory representations continually reinforces and expands upon the evolving understanding of these figures, adding layers of meaning and interpretation far beyond their original mythological context.

The continued popularity of Norse mythology as a whole undoubtedly contributes to this enduring fascination with Valkyries. The inherent ambiguity and lack of extensive detailed accounts within the original texts provided fertile ground for creative interpretation and adaptation. The opportunity to reimagine these figures within modern contexts, to infuse them with contemporary narratives and themes, ensures their continued relevance and ongoing evolution within popular culture. The resulting adaptations constantly push the boundaries of their traditional depiction, enriching the mythology and expanding its resonance across diverse media. The Valkyries, once simply choosers of the slain, have become potent symbols of power, agency, and the complex interplay of fate and free will in modern storytelling. Their evolving image reflects not just a shift in societal attitudes, but a testament to the enduring power and adaptability of ancient mythology itself. The enduring fascination with these figures guarantees that their evolution will continue, shaping and reshaping their image in response to the changing cultural landscape for years to come. The legacy of the Valkyries continues to be actively rewritten, ensuring their ongoing relevance and impact within the realm of modern literature and popular culture.

.

Their depiction in popular media and its impact on public perception

The portrayal of Valkyries in modern media has significantly reshaped public perception, moving them from relatively obscure figures of Norse mythology to iconic symbols of power, beauty, and otherworldly agency. Early representations, often limited to brief mentions in scholarly works or niche fantasy settings, established a foundation of warrior-maidens serving Odin, selecting the slain for Valhalla. However, the advent of popular culture, particularly through video games, film, and literature, dramatically expanded and diversified their image, impacting how the general public understands not only Valkyries themselves, but also the broader context of Norse mythology.

Initially, the relatively limited exposure to Valkyries in popular media often adhered closely to traditional descriptions: fierce, battle-hardened women, riding winged steeds and wielding spears. This depiction, while accurate in reflecting certain aspects of the source material, often lacked depth and nuance. The Valkyries were presented as primarily functional figures, existing solely to fulfill their role in Odin's cosmic order. Their personalities, motivations, and inner lives remained largely unexplored. This simplistic representation, while accessible, unintentionally contributed to a perception of Valkyries as one-dimensional, devoid of the complexity that richer interpretations later revealed.

The rise of fantasy literature and role-playing games played a pivotal role in transforming the popular image of the Valkyries. Authors and game designers imbued them with greater agency and personality, often moving beyond the strictly mythological parameters. This led to more dynamic and relatable characters, sometimes portrayed as compassionate, sometimes merciless, and frequently possessing unique individual stories and motivations beyond their duties to Odin. These narratives challenged the previously held notion of Valkyries as mere instruments of fate, fostering a more empathetic and multifaceted understanding among the public. The ability to interact with these characters, often as allies or adversaries, in interactive media further cemented this shift in perception.

Furthermore, the visual representation of Valkyries evolved dramatically. Early artistic interpretations, often influenced by Romantic ideals, frequently depicted Valkyries with idealized features, emphasizing their beauty over their martial prowess. Modern media, however, embraced a far broader range of aesthetic choices. While the image of the beautiful warrior-maiden remained prevalent, interpretations varied greatly, from grim and battle-scarred figures to ethereal beings of almost supernatural grace. This visual diversity contributed significantly to the public's evolving understanding of their nature, underscoring the inherent flexibility and multifaceted nature of the Valkyrie archetype. The visual appeal, particularly in video games and anime, undeniably played a significant role in popularizing the Valkyries, making them accessible to a wider audience.

The impact of this enhanced visibility and diversification is undeniable. No longer confined to academic circles or specialist fantasy subcultures, Valkyries have become recognizable and widely discussed figures in popular culture. This broader exposure, however, comes with certain caveats. While the more complex portrayals in modern media have enriched public understanding, they have also opened the door to potential misinterpretations and appropriations. The tendency towards romanticizing or sexualizing their image, sometimes evident in certain media productions, represents a deviation from the source material and potentially reinforces harmful stereotypes. Such portrayals can overshadow the original significance of the Valkyries as powerful figures within a rich and complex mythology, potentially trivializing their importance within the context of Norse cosmology.

This complex interplay between accurate representations and creative interpretations highlights the inherent challenge of translating mythological figures into modern media. While the increased visibility and nuanced portrayals have undeniably enhanced public understanding and appreciation of Valkyries, a critical engagement with these representations is vital. The continued need for responsible and accurate depictions is paramount, ensuring that the evolving public perception of these powerful figures remains anchored in a balanced and respectful understanding of their origin and significance within Norse mythology. The ongoing dialogue surrounding their portrayal underscores the significant cultural impact of adapting ancient mythology for modern audiences, demanding a careful balance between artistic license and historical accuracy. The success of this adaptation lies in the ability to foster appreciation for both the original mythological context and the innovative ways in which these timeless figures continue to resonate with contemporary audiences. The ongoing evolution of their image in popular media will continue to shape and redefine public perception for years to come, making this a dynamic and ever-evolving area of study. The challenge lies in ensuring that these evolving interpretations remain both engaging and respectful to the rich tapestry of Norse mythology from which they originated.

.

Chapter 6: Valkyries in Art and Mythology

Artistic representations of Valkyries from ancient times to the present

The artistic representation of Valkyries, those enigmatic figures of Norse mythology, has undergone a fascinating evolution from their ambiguous early depictions to the richly detailed and often romanticized portrayals prevalent today. While direct, verifiable artistic representations from the pre-Christian Norse era are scarce, the surviving artifacts hint at the conceptual framework underpinning later artistic interpretations. The limited imagery found on runestones and in the relatively few surviving artifacts of the Viking Age, such as the Oseberg tapestry, provide tantalizing glimpses, suggesting a focus on the Valkyrie's function as agents of Odin rather than their physical appearance. These early portrayals, often limited to symbolic representations of battle or death, lack the detailed anthropomorphic depictions that would emerge later. The implication of female figures participating in the chaotic and violent world of battle is subtly conveyed, paving the way for more explicit artistic interpretations that would flourish in subsequent centuries.

The absence of detailed visual representations in the Viking Age is arguably less a reflection of their insignificance in Norse cosmology and more a consequence of the limitations of artistic media and the focus on functional rather than purely aesthetic forms. The emphasis in early Norse art was on practical objects, with decorative elements serving largely functional purposes. Artistic expression was often interwoven with practical utility, as seen in intricately carved wood and bone objects or the symbolic patterns on weaponry. The lack of large-scale monumental art, akin to the classical sculpture of Greece or Rome, meant that the potential for detailed and complex representations of Valkyries remained largely untapped during this era. However, the subtle hints at their presence in surviving artifacts— perhaps a stylized female figure amidst a scene of battle, or symbolic imagery associated with death and the afterlife—suggest a latent understanding of their iconic status that would later burst forth into full artistic bloom.

The transition to the post-Viking Age, marked by the increasing influence of Christianity and the subsequent development of a written Norse tradition, saw a significant shift in the artistic depiction of Valkyries. The compilation of Norse mythology into written sagas provided a richer textual framework for artistic interpretations. The literary descriptions, while often fragmented and contradictory, offered artists a more defined narrative to draw upon, moving beyond the purely symbolic representations of the Viking Age. Medieval manuscript illuminations, though not always depicting Valkyries explicitly, sometimes feature female figures engaged in battle scenes or activities associated with death and fate, subtly hinting at the Valkyrie archetype's presence within a broader context of religious or heroic narratives. The influence of contemporary artistic styles, deeply embedded within religious traditions of the time, inevitably shaped how these figures were visually conceptualized.

The Renaissance and subsequent artistic movements brought about a significant change in the artistic treatment of Norse mythology, including the depiction of Valkyries. The rediscovery of classical art and its emphasis on realism and idealized human forms directly influenced artistic interpretations. Valkyries, previously relegated to ancillary roles in broader narratives, began to be depicted as individuals, albeit within the specific framework defined by existing literary sources. The visual vocabulary used to represent them was heavily influenced by the prevailing artistic styles; the idealized beauty of Renaissance and Baroque painting often influenced their depiction as graceful and elegant figures, often contrasted with the brutal reality of warfare. This marked a departure from the more ambiguous representations of the preceding eras, introducing a clearer sense of their physical attributes and aesthetic appeal.

The Romantic era brought about yet another significant shift in the artistic representation of Valkyries. The fascination with the exotic and the sublime, characteristic of this artistic period, heavily impacted their portrayal. Valkyries were increasingly depicted as majestic, ethereal beings, often winged and clad in flowing garments. The Romantic emphasis on emotion and individualism lent itself well to representing the Valkyries' more personal aspects – their choices, their passions, their connections to Odin. The artistic works of this period showcase a deep engagement with the mythological and emotional complexities of the Valkyrie figures, going beyond the simple functional descriptions of earlier eras. This heightened sense of drama and emotional depth added a new layer of complexity to their visual representation.

The 20th and 21st centuries have witnessed a remarkable proliferation of Valkyrie depictions across various media, ranging from illustrations in books and comics to paintings, sculptures, and even film adaptations. The influence of fantasy literature and popular culture has significantly shaped modern portrayals, often incorporating elements from multiple sources and reimagining their roles and appearances. While some artists maintain a degree of fidelity to the traditional characteristics gleaned from older sagas, others take considerable creative liberties, creating unique and often strikingly divergent interpretations. Contemporary artists frequently explore the Valkyries' psychological depth, exploring their motivations, doubts, and conflicts, creating representations that move beyond simple archetypes into complex, nuanced figures. The availability of digital tools and evolving artistic styles further contribute to the ongoing and dynamic evolution of Valkyrie artistic depictions. The Valkyries, once shadowy figures implied rather than explicitly depicted, have become fully realized characters in the artistic imagination, their forms constantly reinterpreted and redefined across centuries of artistic expression. This continued evolution reflects not just the enduring power of Norse mythology, but also the ability of artistic representation to constantly reinvent and reimagine these mythical figures for each successive generation.

.

Symbolism and significance in different artistic mediums

Valkyries, those winged figures of Norse mythology, transcend their narrative origins to become potent symbols readily adapted and reinterpreted across diverse artistic mediums. Their significance shifts subtly yet profoundly depending on the chosen artistic expression, reflecting the enduring power of the myth itself and the artist's individual engagement with its themes. The iconic image of the Valkyrie, often depicted in flight, clad in armor, and wielding a spear, immediately communicates power, agency, and a connection to the supernatural realm. This inherent visual dynamism is exploited in painting and sculpture where the artist can emphasize the Valkyrie's ethereal grace alongside her martial prowess. A painting might employ swirling colors and dynamic brushstrokes to convey the whirlwind of battle from which the Valkyrie selects her fallen, contrasting the chaotic energy of conflict with the serene, almost regal bearing of the figure herself. A sculptor, on the other hand, can manipulate form and texture to convey the Valkyrie's strength and otherworldly nature – the smooth, polished surface of her armor contrasting with the rough, textured wings suggesting both earthly and celestial origins. The very act of choosing, of selecting the worthy from the unworthy, becomes a visual narrative – a sculptor might depict her gaze, focused intently on the battlefield, her spear poised ready to guide a chosen soul to Valhalla, thereby underscoring the weight of her judgment and the power of her divine mandate.

The transition to the graphic arts, specifically illustration and comic books, allows for a different kind of symbolic exploration. The limitations of physical mediums are replaced with the fluidity of line and color. Here, the Valkyrie's symbolism can become more explicit, often conveying specific narrative elements through visual shorthand. The Valkyrie's weaponry can be symbolically laden, the spear itself representing not only a weapon but also a pointer, a guide towards the afterlife. The artist might use specific color palettes to amplify symbolic resonance – deep blues and purples to highlight the Valkyrie's connection to the twilight world and the mysteries of death, or vibrant reds and golds to contrast the brutality of battle with the splendor of Valhalla. The stylistic choices themselves become imbued with meaning; a more realistic depiction might emphasize the Valkyrie's humanity, her connection to the mortal realm, while a more stylized, almost fantastical portrayal can heighten her otherworldly status and amplify her supernatural power. The panels of a comic book can further dissect the Valkyrie's role, presenting her as a detached observer in one panel, a fierce warrior in another, and a compassionate guide in yet another, thereby exploring the multifaceted nature of her being.

The realm of cinema and animation offers even greater possibilities for symbolic exploration. The movement and fluidity of these media permit a visual representation of the Valkyrie's power and grace that transcends the limitations of static art forms. Here, the emphasis shifts from visual symbolism to narrative symbolism. The Valkyrie's flight can be depicted not merely as a physical act but as a symbolic transition between realms – a journey from the chaos of battle to the peace of Valhalla. Sound design and musical score contribute to this symbolic resonance, amplifying the feeling of awe and reverence surrounding the Valkyrie's actions. The selection of a fallen warrior, for instance, can be accompanied by a triumphant fanfare that juxtaposes the death of the warrior with the glory of their passage into the afterlife. Similarly, the depiction of the Valkyrie's own emotions – her sorrow for the slain, her determination in her task, or even her contemplation of mortality – can be profoundly impacting, creating an emotional depth unattainable in static mediums. The choice of lighting, camera angles, and editing further enhance the symbolism, allowing the artist to control the viewer's perception and emotional response, thus manipulating the interpretation of the Valkyrie's role and significance.

In literature, the Valkyrie's symbolic weight often resides in the narrative itself, influencing character development and plot. The Valkyrie can be presented as a figure of fate, an embodiment of inexorable destiny, shaping the lives of mortal characters through her choices. Her presence can create a sense of impending doom or, conversely, hope and redemption, depending on the context of the story. The descriptive language used to depict her appearance, actions, and demeanor further contribute to her symbolic significance. The author's stylistic choices can shape the reader's perception of the Valkyrie, making her a compassionate guardian, a ruthless agent of death, or even a symbol of the unpredictable and uncontrollable forces of fate. Furthermore, the exploration of her own internal conflicts or motivations can add further layers of depth to her symbolism, enabling an exploration of themes such as duty, sacrifice, and the ambiguous nature of divine justice. Metaphorical uses of her image can expand the symbolic horizon, making her a representation of various themes like the inevitability of death, the choice between glory and oblivion, or the enduring power of memory and legacy.

The power of the Valkyrie image, its inherent symbolism and adaptability, makes it a perpetual source of creative inspiration. Across diverse artistic mediums, the Valkyrie's significance evolves, reflecting not only the inherent qualities of the myth but also the individual artistic vision and cultural context of its interpretation. Whether depicted as a fierce warrior, a compassionate guide, or a symbol of the inexorable march of fate, the Valkyrie remains a captivating figure, constantly reimagined and reinterpreted in light of new artistic tools and evolving cultural perspectives. The enduring legacy of this figure rests not only in her narrative potency, but in her persistent capacity to embody and symbolize powerful and enduring human themes. The ongoing evolution of her image in various artistic contexts underlines the richness of the Norse myth and its profound resonance with human experiences, past, present and future. The very act of artistic representation – the constant process of reimagining and reinterpreting the Valkyrie – perpetually revitalizes her symbolic power, ensuring that the legend of the choosers of the slain remains a potent and ever-evolving force in human creativity. The versatility of the imagery ensures its continued relevance, adapting to changing artistic trends and cultural interpretations, demonstrating the remarkable staying power of an ancient myth translated through the lens of modern artistic sensibilities.

.

Chapter 7: Valkyries and Gender

The ambiguous gender roles of Valkyries

The ambiguous nature of Valkyries' gender roles in Norse mythology presents a fascinating area of study, defying simple categorization and challenging modern expectations of rigidly defined gender binaries. While often depicted as female warriors, their roles extend far beyond the battlefield, blurring the lines between traditionally masculine and feminine spheres of influence in a way that resists straightforward interpretation. Their agency in choosing the slain, a power seemingly at odds with the passive roles often ascribed to women in other mythological contexts, demands a nuanced understanding of their position within the Norse cosmology. The Valkyries are not simply female fighters; their selection of those destined for Valhalla or Hel implies a level of judgment and authority traditionally associated with male figures of power in many cultures. This capacity for decisive action, often involving the determination of life and death, fundamentally complicates any attempt to confine them within a conventional gender paradigm.

Furthermore, their association with Odin, the all-father, highlights the intricate power dynamics at play. Serving as his messengers and handmaidens, they participate directly in his divine activities, suggesting a level of intimacy and influence that surpasses the typical societal boundaries imposed upon women in many cultures' mythological frameworks. This close relationship with a supreme male deity could be interpreted in multiple ways: as a subordination reinforcing traditional gender hierarchies, or alternatively, as a demonstration of the exceptional power granted to these figures, transcending the limitations normally placed upon females. The ambiguity lies precisely in the potential for both readings, making any simplistic assertion about their subordinate status problematic. Their function within Odin's court defies easy classification: are they his obedient servants, or powerful agents operating within his sphere of influence with significant autonomy? The textual evidence supports both interpretations, highlighting the intentional ambiguity that imbues the myths themselves.

The depiction of Valkyries in visual art and literary sources further complicates the issue. While often portrayed in armor and wielding weapons, showcasing a warrior ethos traditionally attributed to men, their representations also frequently contain elements emphasizing their beauty and grace, traits often associated with femininity. This simultaneous display of both martial strength and alluring physical characteristics is not contradictory, but instead emphasizes the multiplicity inherent within their characterization. It suggests a deliberate blurring of conventional gender aesthetics, deliberately defying simple binary oppositions, and prompting a reconsideration of how gender is expressed and understood within the context of Norse mythology. Are these visual representations simply reflecting a societal desire to reconcile the seemingly incompatible traits of warrior and woman, or are they actively subversively dismantling preconceived notions of female capability? The answer is likely nuanced and depends on the interpretation of the specific artistic expression, underlining the inherent ambiguity present within the material.

The narrative structure itself contributes to the ambiguous presentation of Valkyrie gender roles. The stories concerning Valkyries often lack a single, consistent portrayal. In some instances, they appear as fearsome warriors, engaged in direct combat, displaying strength and prowess typically associated with masculine heroes. In other narratives, their role emphasizes their capacity for choosing and guiding fallen warriors, suggesting a more ethereal and symbolic power, one that could be argued leans toward traditionally feminine archetypes of nurturer and guide. The shifting presentation across different myths underscores the inherent complexity and resists a singular, definitive interpretation of their gender roles. This lack of uniformity is not a flaw in the mythological tradition, but rather a key element contributing to their lasting appeal and ongoing scholarly debate.

The language used to describe Valkyries further emphasizes this fluidity. The words used to describe them in Old Norse texts often contain a double-edged quality, capable of conveying both strength and beauty, courage and grace. These nuanced descriptions, intentionally avoiding simple categorization, reflect a deliberate ambiguity in the myths themselves, showcasing a deliberate challenge to fixed gender roles. The lack of easily applicable labels or classifications reflects the sophisticated understanding of gender that may have been present in Norse society, an understanding far more complex than often reflected in simplified interpretations of their mythology. The richness of language employed highlights the inherent richness and sophistication of the mythological construct. The ambiguous nature of Valkyrie gender roles highlights not a lack of clarity in the myths, but rather a sophisticated understanding of gender's complexities.

The enduring fascination with Valkyries stems, in part, from this inherent ambiguity. Their characters resist easy categorization and continue to challenge and inspire reinterpretations. This enduring power lies in their capacity to transcend simplistic definitions and embody a spectrum of qualities typically associated with both masculinity and femininity, inviting ongoing critical analysis and interpretation. The multiplicity embedded within their portrayals allows for a multifaceted understanding of gender that remains both relevant and insightful in contemporary society. Their very ambiguity, far from being a weakness, serves as a testament to the sophistication and complexity of the Norse worldview, one that recognized and embraced the fluidity of gender roles rather than confining them within rigid societal structures. Their continued presence in modern popular culture is a testament to the enduring power and appeal of this ambiguity, prompting a continual re-evaluation of our own understanding of gender.

.

Their portrayal as female warriors and as divine attendants

The portrayal of Valkyries in Norse mythology presents a fascinating paradox: they are simultaneously fierce warriors and ethereal divine attendants, a duality that complicates simplistic gender roles and challenges conventional understandings of power within the mythological framework. Their existence transcends the limitations often imposed on women within patriarchal societies, showcasing agency and strength in a manner rarely paralleled in comparable mythologies. This dual identity is not merely a juxtaposition but rather a complex interplay, where their martial prowess reinforces their divine status, and their divine authority underpins their battlefield capabilities. The Valkyries' battlefield roles, choosing the slain to join Odin in Valhalla, are not merely passive acts of selection but represent a profound involvement in the very fabric of fate and cosmic order. This active participation in the cycle of death and rebirth positions them as agents of change, wielding influence over the ultimate destinies of warriors. The very act of choosing, a seemingly passive function, implicitly grants them power over life and death within the context of the Norse cosmology.

Their warrior aspect transcends mere participation; they are depicted actively engaged in combat, often depicted riding into battle, armed and armored, sometimes even leading troops into the fray. This depiction directly contradicts the limitations traditionally placed upon women in many societies, demonstrating a disregard for societal norms and expectations. Their combat prowess is not a separate entity from their divine role, but rather an integral part of it. They are not merely fighting for the sake of fighting, but rather acting as extensions of Odin's will, executing his divine judgment and shaping the battlefield's outcome. The imagery of the Valkyries, clad in gleaming armor and wielding spears, reinforces their power and agency, visually representing their active participation in the violent chaos of war. Their very appearance—often described as strikingly beautiful even amidst the carnage—further emphasizes this duality, suggesting a potent blend of feminine allure and formidable martial skill. This potent combination underscores the complex nature of their character, defying simplistic categorization and highlighting the multifaceted nature of power within the Norse pantheon.

Further examining their role as divine attendants reveals a nuanced understanding of their power. They are not simply servants or handmaidens, but rather integral members of Odin's court, entrusted with vital duties that directly impact the cosmic order. Their participation in the feasts of Valhalla reinforces their close relationship with Odin and the other gods, signifying a level of intimacy and trust not usually afforded to secondary figures. This proximity to the divine suggests a level of authority and influence that transcends their battlefield roles. The description of them serving mead and attending to the Einherjar, the chosen warriors of Valhalla, showcases their responsibility and involvement in the afterlife. This responsibility is not merely logistical; it signifies their role in maintaining the balance between the mortal and divine realms, a task of cosmic significance that underlines their status within the mythological framework. Their very presence in Valhalla, the hall of the slain, further reinforces their power—a power that stems from their active role in shaping the very composition of this sacred space.

The blending of their divine status and martial abilities highlights their exceptional position within the Norse pantheon and societal constructs. Unlike other female figures in Norse mythology, who are frequently relegated to more passive roles, the Valkyries actively shape events, influence destinies, and wield significant power. This active participation in the shaping of both the mortal and divine realms makes their representation exceptionally unique, illustrating a complexity rarely seen in other mythological female figures. Their portrayal is not merely a depiction of women in battle, but rather a complex exploration of power, fate, and the dynamic interplay between the human and divine worlds. They embody a sophisticated understanding of gender roles within a context that simultaneously embraces and challenges traditional societal structures. The very existence of

Valkyries, with their inherent duality, questions the simplistic categorization of gender and power within the broader framework of Norse mythology, creating a rich tapestry of multifaceted characterizations that continue to intrigue and fascinate. The sustained interest in their mythology speaks to the enduring power of their image, a captivating blend of feminine grace and deadly prowess, forever etched into the annals of Norse legend. The enduring legacy of the Valkyries underscores their enduring importance and impact on our understanding of Norse mythology, continually provoking new interpretations and perspectives.

.

Chapter 8: Valkyries and Destiny

The role of Valkyries in shaping human destiny

The Valkyries, in Norse mythology, transcend mere battlefield attendants; they are active agents in the shaping of human destiny, wielding a power that intertwines the mortal and divine realms. Their role extends far beyond the simple selection of slain warriors for Valhalla. While their participation in the selection of those who fall gloriously in battle is undeniable, a deeper analysis reveals a far more nuanced and intricate influence on the course of human lives, both individual and collective. The very act of choosing, itself, implies a pre-ordained plan, a cosmic tapestry woven by the Valkyries' selections, impacting not just the afterlife of the chosen, but also the living, the battles fought, and even the overall flow of history. The narrative surrounding their choices is seldom presented as arbitrary; rather, it suggests a deliberate orchestration to fulfill larger prophecies or to maintain the cosmic balance. A warrior's valor, indeed his very fate, becomes intrinsically linked to the Valkyries' judgment, highlighting the crucial role they play in the Norse concept of fate, or wyrd. They are not merely passive observers of the battlefield but active participants, shaping the very fabric of existence through their discerning choices. The chosen warriors, by virtue of their selection, become imbued with a heightened significance, their deaths contributing not just to the glory of Odin, but to the ongoing narrative of the cosmos itself. The very act of a Valkyrie's selection elevates the slain beyond mere mortality; it transforms them into symbols of strength, honor, and the very essence of Norse heroic ideals, influencing future generations through the tales that would be spun about their legendary feats. This, in turn, impacts the cultural narrative, shaping the values and aspirations of the living. Their choices, therefore, have a ripple effect, influencing the very fabric of Norse society and belief.

The ambiguity surrounding the Valkyries' agency further complicates their role in shaping destiny. Are they simply instruments of a higher power, carrying out pre-determined choices, or do they possess a degree of independent judgment and the capacity to influence the outcome of battles and the fate of individuals? The myths themselves offer conflicting narratives, leaving room for interpretation and enriching the complexity of their function. Some accounts depict them as obedient servants of Odin, their choices reflecting his pre-ordained plan. Others, however, suggest a greater degree of autonomy, indicating their capacity for personal judgment and even intervention. This ambiguity underscores their significance; their actions are not simply the execution of divine will, but a dynamic interaction between the divine and the mortal realms, a subtle interplay that constantly shapes and reshapes the course of events. Their involvement in weaving the tapestry of wyrd is not a passive one; they are active participants in the unfolding of fate, their choices subtly but profoundly impacting the course of battles, the rise and fall of kingdoms, and the very destiny of nations. The unpredictability inherent in their agency adds a layer of mystique to their role, reinforcing their status as powerful and enigmatic figures within the Norse pantheon. Their choices are not easily deciphered, implying a hidden logic that surpasses mere human understanding. This reinforces the underlying concept of wyrd, the inescapable, yet often mysterious, thread of fate that binds all beings in the Norse cosmology.

The visual imagery associated with the Valkyries further emphasizes their role in shaping destiny. Their winged steeds, their shining armor, and their ethereal beauty all contribute to their portrayal as powerful and otherworldly beings, capable of bridging the gap between the realms of the living and the dead. Their flight across the battlefields is not simply a means of transporting the slain; it symbolizes the movement of fate itself, a relentless force that carries individuals towards their predetermined destinies. Their very appearance on the battlefield can be interpreted as an omen, a foreshadowing of events to come, influencing the course of the conflict and the decisions made by the warriors themselves. The descriptions of their actions, often infused with poetic language and symbolic imagery, highlight the significance of their choices and their impact on both the immediate outcome of battles and the broader narrative of human existence. This potent visual language deepens their mythical status and underscores their ability to manipulate and control the flow of events, transforming them from mere choosers of the slain into active architects of fate. The descriptions, therefore, are not simply narrations of events, but powerful symbols that convey the extent of their influence and their fundamental role in the shaping of human destiny within the Norse mythological framework. Their imagery becomes a conduit, translating the abstract concept of wyrd into a visually striking and emotionally resonant narrative.

The Valkyries' connection to the gods, particularly Odin, further enhances their influence on human destiny. Their role as messengers and intermediaries underscores their capacity to transmit divine will and to shape the course of events in accordance with a higher plan. The fact that they serve Odin, the Allfather, places them at the apex of the Norse pantheon, granting them access to knowledge and power that transcends human comprehension. Their proximity to Odin suggests that their choices are not merely based on individual merit but reflect a broader cosmic strategy, contributing to the larger purpose of the gods and the maintenance of the cosmos. The lines between their individual agency and the divine plan often blur, highlighting the intertwined nature of fate and free will within the Norse cosmology. This blurring underscores the complex interplay between human actions and divine intervention, suggesting that while humans have the capacity to shape their own destinies, they remain subject to the larger forces that govern the universe, forces that the Valkyries actively channel and manipulate. This interplay emphasizes the idea that destiny is not a fixed and immutable entity, but rather a dynamic and evolving process, constantly shaped and reshaped by the actions of both mortals and gods, with the Valkyries acting as crucial intermediaries in this intricate process. Their actions, therefore, represent a vital link between the human and divine realms, highlighting the interconnectedness of all existence within the Norse worldview. It is through this connection that the Valkyries acquire their profound power, acting as conduits of divine will and shaping the very course of human history.

.

Their connection to the Fates and the cycles of life and death

The Valkyries, those winged maidens of Norse myth, stand as potent intermediaries between the mortal realm and the divine, their roles intricately woven into the very fabric of life, death, and destiny, echoing and expanding upon the functions of the Norns, the Fates of Norse cosmology. Unlike the relatively static, though powerful, Norns who primarily spin, measure, and cut the thread of life, the Valkyries are dynamic agents of fate, actively shaping the course of events, particularly on the battlefields of the gods. Their agency lies not in predestination alone, but in selection, a crucial element distinguishing their function from that of the Fates. The Norns determine the length of life; the Valkyries, in a sense, choose how that life ends, and consequently, where the soul journeys afterward. This active participation, this choosing of the slain, positions the Valkyries as executors of the Norns' decree, adding a layer of active, dynamic judgment to the otherwise seemingly inevitable unfolding of fate.

The connection deepens when considering the Valkyries' selection process. They are not simply arbiters of death, indiscriminately collecting souls. Their choices, though often shrouded in the mists of prophecy and divine whim, reflect a nuanced understanding of valor, skill, and ultimately, the worthiness of a warrior's life in the grand cosmic scheme. This suggests a degree of moral judgment embedded within the seemingly impersonal mechanics of fate. The warrior's death, chosen by a Valkyrie, is not merely an end, but a transition, a validation of a life lived according to certain ideals—ideals that resonate with the broader themes of heroic sacrifice and the upholding of cosmic order embedded within Norse cosmology. The fallen warrior, chosen by a Valkyrie, is not just a casualty, but a participant in a larger, predetermined narrative of destiny, actively contributing to the ongoing conflict between the gods and the forces of chaos.

The cyclical nature of life and death, a central tenet of Norse belief, is explicitly mirrored in the Valkyries' activities. Their selection of the slain ensures the continuation of the cycle. Those chosen find themselves in Valhalla or Folkvangr, halls of the slain where they await the final battle of Ragnarök. This suggests that death, in the context of the Valkyries' actions, is not a termination, but rather a necessary stage in the grand, overarching cycle, a transition fueling the next iteration of the conflict. Their actions are not merely the execution of predetermined fate, but active participation in its perpetuation, ensuring the continued unfolding of destiny. The slain warriors, gathered by the Valkyries, become integral components in the inevitable final clash, further demonstrating the interconnectedness between the Valkyries' choices and the cyclical nature of the Norse cosmos.

Moreover, the Valkyries' connection to the gods, primarily Odin, underscores their role in maintaining the cosmic order. They are not independent agents of fate, but rather extensions of the divine will, acting upon the larger, overarching plan of the gods, itself tied intrinsically to the threads spun by the Norns. This highlights a hierarchical structure: the Norns determine the duration of life, Odin, or perhaps the broader pantheon, sets the overall cosmic narrative, and the Valkyries act as agents of execution, ensuring the destined outcome. Their connection to the gods, therefore, underscores their position as pivotal participants in the larger cosmological drama, where the destinies of individuals are intricately interwoven with the fate of the gods themselves.

The seemingly arbitrary nature of some Valkyrie choices also hints at a deeper, perhaps unknowable, aspect of fate. While valor and skill often appear to be the determining factors, the element of divine whim suggests that fate, even within the well-defined parameters established by the Norns, contains unpredictable elements. This suggests that the Valkyries, despite their apparent agency, are also subject to forces beyond their own understanding, mirroring the inherent unpredictability woven into the fabric of fate itself. This adds a layer of complexity to their role, reminding us that while they participate actively in the unfolding of destiny, they are not its sole architects, highlighting the interwoven nature of divine will, preordained fate, and the unpredictable currents of the cosmos.

They are not simply reapers, but choosers, shaping the narrative of fate by selectively guiding the souls of the fallen. Their choices, though seemingly arbitrary at times, reflect the complex interplay of valor, divine will, and the overarching cyclical nature of the Norse cosmos. Their function, therefore, transcends the mere execution of fate; they actively participate in its ongoing perpetuation, ensuring the continuous flow of life, death, and the inevitable coming of Ragnarök, the ultimate culmination of the cosmic cycle. Their actions serve as a constant reminder of the intricate tapestry of destiny woven by the Norns, meticulously executed by the Valkyries, and ultimately overseen by the gods.

.

Chapter 9: Valkyries and Supernatural Beings

Valkyries' interactions with other supernatural entities in Norse mythology

Valkyries, the choosers of the slain, occupy a fascinating and complex niche within the Norse pantheon, their interactions with other supernatural entities woven intricately into the very fabric of Norse mythology. Their role as intermediaries between the mortal and divine realms necessitates a multifaceted engagement with a vast array of supernatural beings, revealing a dynamic power structure and a nuanced understanding of cosmic order. Their relationships are rarely straightforward alliances or outright hostilities; instead, they exhibit a spectrum of interactions shaped by circumstance, individual agency, and the inherent ambiguities within the Norse cosmological system. The very nature of their task – selecting worthy warriors to populate Odin's hall of Valhalla – places them in constant contact with the Einherjar, the chosen fallen warriors themselves. This isn't a simple employer-employee relationship; the Valkyries' choices directly impact the composition and power of Odin's army, influencing the outcome of future conflicts and even the fate of the gods themselves. The Valkyries' selection process, often depicted as a fierce and glorious battle on the field of carnage, implies a level of engagement with the forces of death and destruction themselves, suggesting an understanding, perhaps even a degree of manipulation, of the very energies that fuel the cycle of violence and rebirth inherent in Norse cosmology.

Their connections extend beyond the Einherjar to encompass the broader supernatural landscape. Interactions with the Norns, the three fate-weavers, are subtly implied but profoundly significant. While not explicitly depicted as direct interactions, the Valkyries' choices undoubtedly intersect with the Norns' predetermined destinies. The Valkyries' selection process cannot be entirely independent of the Norns' weaving; their decisions are constrained, yet they also possess a degree of agency, suggesting a complex interplay between predetermined fate and individual choice within the Norse supernatural world. This subtle tension hints at a delicate balance of power between these potent female figures, a dance between the pre-ordained and the emergent, reflecting the nuanced understanding of fate and free will prevalent in Norse mythology. The implication is one of collaborative influence rather than outright conflict, a shared responsibility in the shaping of destiny.

Further complexity arises from their relationship with other powerful female figures in Norse mythology. The interactions, often alluded to rather than explicitly described, suggest a spectrum of relationships from cooperation to rivalry. The connection with the dísir, female spirits associated with ancestral worship and fertility, suggests a shared domain of influence over the lives and deaths of mortals. This overlap in their responsibilities may imply both collaboration and potential conflict, highlighting the inherent complexities of power dynamics within the female supernatural sphere. Consideration of the Valkyries' potential interactions with powerful female giants, such as the völva or seeresses, offers further possibilities for nuanced engagements. Their shared knowledge of hidden things and the fates of mortals could lead to alliances based on mutual advantage, perhaps even a shared respect born from the understanding of their respective positions within the complex supernatural hierarchy. However, the inherent power dynamics between the goddesses and the giantesses could just as easily lead to conflict or tense neutrality, mirroring the volatile relationships often seen within the pantheon as a whole.

The Valkyries' interactions with the gods themselves, particularly Odin, are central to their narrative function. While serving as Odin's messengers and agents, their role is not simply one of subservience. Their choices, their agency in selecting warriors, represent a form of power negotiation within the divine hierarchy. This is not a straightforward master-servant dynamic;

instead, it hints at a more complex relationship of mutual dependence, wherein the Valkyries' contributions are integral to Odin's power and strategic objectives. Their association with Odin also places them in indirect contact with other Aesir gods, although these interactions are less frequently depicted. The possibility of interactions with Thor, the god of thunder, during battles or after the fall of a chosen warrior presents a compelling narrative opportunity. Similarly, interactions with Freyja, goddess of love and war, whose own hall, Fólkvangr, receives half of the slain, reveals a direct competitor in their shared sphere of influence over the fate of fallen warriors. This suggests a potential for rivalry, collaboration, or even a complex negotiation of power and influence, reflecting the fluid and multi-layered nature of the Norse supernatural world.

Beyond the more prominent figures, the Valkyries' interactions extend to lesser-known entities of the Norse cosmological landscape. Their travels across battlefields and into the realms of the dead imply potential encounters with various types of spirits, ghosts, or other supernatural beings that inhabit the liminal spaces between the worlds. These encounters, often left to implication and interpretation, contribute to the overall sense of mystery and awe surrounding the Valkyries' role and the intricate web of supernatural forces within Norse mythology. The very act of traversing realms and witnessing the carnage of battle exposes the Valkyries to a multitude of supernatural energies and influences. These encounters, even if only alluded to, add further layers of complexity to their characterization, illustrating their position as active participants in a vast and interconnected supernatural realm. The possibility of interactions with mischievous or malevolent entities—the various forms of trolls, giants, or even mischievous spirits—adds further depth and potential conflict to their story. The subtle implication of these encounters underlines the inherent dangers and unpredictable nature of their task, revealing a world where the lines between benevolent and malevolent forces are often blurred and their agency tested at every turn. Their survival and continued efficacy as choosers of the slain underscores their inherent skill, strength, and cunning within a hostile and unpredictable supernatural environment. They are not merely passive messengers; they are active agents navigating a treacherous landscape of supernatural power, constantly negotiating their position and wielding their influence within the complex and often volatile hierarchy of Norse mythology.

.

Their relationships with Odin, Thor, and other gods

The Valkyries' relationship with the Norse pantheon, particularly Odin, Thor, and others, is a complex tapestry woven from threads of duty, subservience, and, at times, subtle defiance. Their primary allegiance undeniably rests with Odin, the Allfather, who commands and empowers them. They are his handmaidens, his agents of death, tasked with selecting the slain on battlefields and guiding worthy warriors to Valhalla, his glorious hall. This selection process itself highlights a subtle power dynamic; while ostensibly acting on Odin's orders, the Valkyries possess a degree of agency in determining who merits entry into the afterlife's most prestigious realm. Their choices aren't merely mechanical, reflecting a nuanced understanding of warrior prowess beyond mere battlefield statistics. They perceive valor, courage, and adherence to a specific warrior code, demonstrating a judgment independent of Odin's direct supervision, albeit within the framework of his overarching will. This implies a level of trust and respect afforded to the Valkyries, recognizing their innate abilities to discern true heroic merit.

The bond between Odin and the Valkyries transcends a simple master-servant dynamic. Their connection is imbued with a mystical, almost familial element. They are frequently depicted as his daughters, or at least closely related, reflecting an intimate understanding and a shared participation in the maintenance of cosmic order. Odin's power directly fuels their abilities; they ride winged steeds, possess supernatural insight, and wield formidable weaponry, all gifts bestowed by him. However, the Valkyries are not mere passive recipients of power. Their actions actively contribute to the fulfillment of Odin's greater designs. They gather warriors for his army, ensuring the continued strength and vitality of Valhalla, strengthening Odin's dominion over the afterlife and, by extension, the living world. This active participation in Odin's plans demonstrates a dynamic reciprocal relationship, a mutual dependence that strengthens the power structure of Asgard as a whole. The Valkyries are not simply tools; they are integral components of Odin's cosmic machinery.

While Odin occupies the central position in their divine relationships, Thor's presence in their lives is less direct but nonetheless significant. The God of Thunder is primarily associated with earthly battles and the protection of Asgard, engaging in direct conflict while the Valkyries operate on a more metaphysical plane. However, their paths inevitably intersect on the battlefields where Thor fights. Their selection process directly impacts the outcome of his battles, influencing the balance of power between gods and monsters, and between mortal kingdoms. The Valkyries' choices shape the strength of the armies he encounters, either bolstering or diminishing the ranks of his foes. This indirect influence highlights a subtle interconnectedness between their roles and the overall success of Asgard's earthly defenders. Though not a direct command structure, a symbiotic connection exists: Thor's successes are indirectly augmented by the Valkyries' selective gathering of worthy warriors, while their role is indirectly enhanced by the ongoing struggles and victories that provide them with their charge.

Beyond Odin and Thor, the Valkyries' interactions with other gods are less frequently documented but nonetheless imply a broader web of relationships within the Norse pantheon. Their role in shaping the flow of souls into the afterlife necessarily places them within the complex cosmological order orchestrated by the Aesir and Vanir. Their actions impact the balance of power in the nine realms, influencing not only the mortal world but also the realms of the gods themselves. The subtle undercurrents of their involvement suggest an awareness of, and participation in, the broader godly intrigues and struggles, even if their actions remain primarily focused on the collection of the fallen. While specific interactions with other deities might be less detailed in surviving lore, the implied connection indicates a broader tapestry of relationships that extends beyond their direct links to Odin and Thor. Their presence transcends singular relationships; they occupy a unique space within the Norse cosmos, acting as a bridge between the realms of the living and the dead, subtly influencing the fortunes of gods and mortals alike. The Valkyries' profound and intricate involvement in the Norse mythological framework is far from simple servitude; it represents a complex interplay of power, duty, and agency within the broader divine structure.

.

Chapter 10: Valkyries in Ritual and Practice

Rituals and practices associated with Valkyries in Norse culture

The paucity of direct, explicit sources detailing Valkyrie rituals and practices necessitates a nuanced approach, drawing inferences from broader Norse religious practices and extrapolating from the limited textual and archaeological evidence available. While the Valkyries themselves are not depicted participating directly in documented rituals in the same way as, say, the Aesir or Vanir gods, their role as choosers of the slain implies a profound, albeit indirect, involvement in funerary rites and the broader understanding of death and afterlife in Norse society. Their function as intermediaries between the battlefield and the afterlife suggests a blurring of the lines between the human and divine realms, where ritual acts, though not performed by the Valkyries, were intrinsically linked to their sphere of influence.

The very act of dying gloriously in battle, a prerequisite for selection by the Valkyries, itself constituted a ritualized action. Warriors adorned themselves for battle, performing acts of personal devotion and invoking their gods for protection and victory. This preparation was not merely practical, but a form of ritual self-sacrifice, a dedication of one's life to the glory of Odin and the ensuing afterlife in Valhalla. The warrior's death, then, becomes a culminating ritual act, not merely an ending, but a transition facilitated, albeit unseen, by the Valkyries. The battlefield itself, strewn with the slain and marked by the clash of arms, became a liminal space, a threshold between worlds. The Valkyries, existing within this liminal zone, acted as guides through this crucial transition.

The subsequent funerary rites, though not directly attributed to the Valkyries, were certainly influenced by their presence in the mythological framework. The elaborate ship burials, replete with grave goods reflecting the deceased's social standing and achievements, may be interpreted as a reflection of the warrior's aspiration to gain the Valkyries' favor. The inclusion of weapons, armour, and even sacrificed animals, might be seen as offerings not only to the gods but also to ensure a successful passage into the afterlife orchestrated by these divine choosers. The ritualistic nature of the funeral pyre, the symbolic burning of the body, could further be viewed as a theatrical representation of the journey undertaken under the Valkyries' guidance, a fiery passage to the hall of Odin.

The lack of direct textual description of Valkyrie-specific rituals allows for interpretative possibilities. Considering the prominence of seidr, a form of Norse shamanistic practice, it is tempting to speculate on the Valkyries' potential involvement in rituals related to divination and prophecy. Seidr practitioners were often associated with accessing otherworldly realms, and the Valkyries' ability to observe and choose warriors suggests a similar connection to visionary realms. This hypothetical link does not posit a direct ritualistic role for the Valkyries in seidr practices, but rather hints at a possible overlap between the practices of seidr and the broader cosmological context in which the Valkyries operate.

The close association of the Valkyries with Odin, the Allfather, further underscores their implicit role in ritual. Odin's own practices, including his self-sacrifice on Yggdrasil and his frequent communion with the supernatural, establish a precedent for ritual actions deeply connected to the afterlife and divine intervention. The Valkyries, as Odin's handmaidens, would naturally occupy a space within this overarching ritual framework, even if their participation is not explicitly documented. Their image, often depicted on runestones and artifacts, served as a reminder of this divine connection and perhaps acted as a visual invocation during more personal funerary rituals or acts of devotion.

The pervasive presence of the Valkyries in Norse mythology and associated imagery, despite the absence of detailed ritual descriptions, highlights their significance within the broader religious and cultural context. Their implicit role in the transition from life to death—from battlefield to Valhalla—makes them integral to the funerary rituals and the warrior ethos of Norse society. The very acts performed around the death and burial of a warrior, the choices made in the creation of the burial mounds and the inclusion of specific grave goods, can all be viewed through the lens of attempting to secure the Valkyries' favor and ensuring a successful passage into the afterlife. The lack of explicit ritual documentation is not necessarily an indication of the Valkyries' insignificance; instead, it underlines the subtle and pervasive manner in which their influence was woven into the fabric of Norse beliefs and practices. The subtle power of the Valkyries' presence lay in their ability to shape the context of life and death, making the rituals surrounding these pivotal moments deeply imbued with their ethereal power. The rituals themselves, therefore, become a testament to the profound impact of the Valkyries' influence, even in the absence of directly documented Valkyrie-led ceremonies. Their power was felt in the preparations for battle, in the glorious deaths they selected, and in the rituals performed to honor those who met their end under their watchful gaze. The very act of choosing the slain was, in itself, the most profound ritual action of all.

.

The significance of invoking Valkyries for protection and guidance

The invocation of Valkyries for protection and guidance transcends mere mythological curiosity; it speaks to a deeply ingrained human need for solace, security, and divinely ordained assistance in navigating the perilous uncertainties of life. Within the context of Norse belief, this invocation wasn't a whimsical act but a profoundly serious ritual, laden with implications for both the individual and the wider community. The Valkyries, far from being mere passive observers of battle, were active agents of fate, capable of shaping outcomes and influencing the destinies of mortals. Therefore, appealing to them was not simply a prayer for good fortune, but an attempt to actively engage with the very fabric of existence, to align oneself with the powerful currents of fate channeled through these ethereal beings. The significance lies not only in the potential benefits – protection in battle, successful hunting, a favorable outcome in a feud – but also in the underlying philosophical commitment to a worldview where the gods, and their intermediaries like the Valkyries, actively participate in human affairs. This belief instilled a sense of connection to a larger cosmic order, mitigating the fear of the unknown and providing a framework for understanding both prosperity and adversity. The act of invocation, meticulously performed with appropriate offerings and invocations, represented a profound act of faith, a declaration of reliance on forces beyond human control, yet potentially manipulable through ritual and reverence.

The protective aspect of Valkyrie invocation extended beyond physical safety. Their guidance encompassed a wider spectrum of life's challenges, encompassing not only battlefield survival but also prosperity, successful ventures, and even spiritual guidance. The Valkyries, as choosers of the slain, held a unique position of influence over the transition between life and death. Seeking their favor, therefore, implied a desire not only for continued life but also for a favorable passage into the afterlife, a transition smoothed by their benevolent intervention. This extended protection went beyond simple physical invulnerability; it encompassed the broader concept of well-being, encompassing mental fortitude, spiritual strength, and the ability to navigate complex social and political landscapes. In a world rife with conflict and uncertainty, the promise of Valkyrie protection offered an invaluable psychological anchor, imbuing individuals with a sense of purpose and resilience in the face of adversity. This inherent psychological strength, fostered by the belief in Valkyrie intervention, was arguably as significant as any physical protection they might offer. The very act of seeking their aid served as a potent affirmation of faith, reinforcing the individual's connection to the wider cosmic order and bolstering their inner resolve.

Furthermore, the invocation of Valkyries wasn't merely a private affair. It often integrated into communal practices, reflecting the deeply interwoven nature of individual and societal well-being within Norse culture. Collective invocations, performed before battles or during periods of communal crisis, solidified social bonds and fostered a sense of shared destiny. The shared act of seeking Valkyrie protection served as a potent symbol of unity, reinforcing social cohesion and bolstering morale. These collective rituals weren't simply about obtaining tangible benefits; they served a vital function in maintaining social order, reinforcing cultural values, and affirming the shared belief system that underpinned Norse society. The efficacy of the invocation was intrinsically linked to the community's faith and shared commitment to the ritual's purpose, transforming it into a powerful force for social cohesion and collective resilience. The collective invocation of the Valkyries created a powerful feedback loop, where individual faith reinforced community strength, and communal belief enhanced the individual's conviction and sense of security. This interconnectedness is a crucial element in understanding the significance of Valkyrie invocation in Norse culture.

The significance of invoking Valkyries extends beyond the practical aspects of protection and guidance. It also speaks to the deeper spiritual and philosophical underpinnings of Norse mythology. The Valkyries represented the bridge between the human and divine realms, embodying the capricious nature of fate and the powerful influence of the gods in human lives. Their role in choosing the slain highlighted the inherent uncertainty of existence and the importance of acknowledging the forces beyond human control. Therefore, invoking them wasn't merely a pragmatic attempt to improve one's chances of survival or success; it was an act of profound spiritual engagement, a recognition of the precariousness of life and a humble acceptance of the gods' ultimate power. This acceptance, far from being passive resignation, imbued the invocation with a profound sense of meaning and purpose, transforming a potentially desperate plea for assistance into an affirmation of faith and a conscious alignment with the cosmic order. This act of conscious engagement with the divine, manifested through the invocation of Valkyries, served as a powerful mechanism for coping with life's inherent anxieties and uncertainties.

The enduring appeal of Valkyrie invocation stems from its capacity to address fundamental human needs – the need for security, guidance, and a sense of connection to something larger than oneself. In a world characterized by uncertainty and unpredictable forces, the belief in powerful divine intermediaries capable of influencing fate offered solace and hope. The Valkyries, with their potent symbolism and ethereal presence, became powerful figures of both fear and reverence, capable of inspiring both awe and profound devotion. The act of invoking them transcended simple superstition; it was a complex ritual that touched upon the deepest aspects of the human psyche, providing a framework for understanding the world, navigating its complexities, and finding strength in the face of adversity. The persistence of their presence in modern Norse paganism and popular culture testifies to the enduring power of their mythos, the continued relevance of their symbolic significance, and the persistent human need for guidance and protection in a world that often feels chaotic and unpredictable. The invocation of the Valkyries, therefore, remains a potent symbol of human faith, resilience, and the enduring quest for meaning and purpose in a vast and often bewildering universe.

Chapter 11: Valkyrie Traditions and Customs

Cultural customs and traditions surrounding Valkyries

The cultural customs and traditions surrounding Valkyries in Norse mythology are complex and multifaceted, woven into the very fabric of their existence as intermediaries between the mortal and divine realms. Their role as choosers of the slain is not merely a grim task, but a reflection of a deeply ingrained societal structure that values martial prowess and heroic death. The selection process itself, far from being arbitrary, suggests a nuanced understanding of honor and valor. A Valkyrie's judgment, influenced by Odin's will but shaped by their own perception of a warrior's worth, embodies a complex interplay of fate and meritocracy. The warrior's conduct in battle, their adherence to oaths and codes of honor, their display of courage and skill – all contribute to the Valkyrie's assessment, highlighting a societal reverence for honorable combat and a distinct hierarchy within the battlefield pantheon.

Beyond their battlefield duties, Valkyrie culture demonstrates a unique blend of ethereal grace and martial prowess. Their attire, often described as shimmering armor interwoven with celestial fabrics, reflects this duality. The imagery suggests not just protection in battle, but a connection to the supernatural realms they inhabit. Their weaponry, whether spears or swords, is not merely functional but symbolically charged, imbued with the power of Odin and the weight of their divine mandate. Furthermore, their mounts – often described as swift, winged steeds – reinforce their otherworldly status, underscoring their ability to traverse the gap between the mortal world and the hall of Odin, Valhalla. The speed and grace of their steeds mirror the swiftness and precision of their judgment, further emphasizing their role as agents of divine justice on the battlefield.

The Valkyries' feasting rituals in Valhalla offer another glimpse into their cultural customs. These are not simply meals, but sacred ceremonies that reinforce the bonds between the Valkyries and the chosen slain warriors. The act of serving mead and food to the Einherjar is a ritualistic affirmation of their heroic deeds, a celebration of their valor and a sanctification of their deaths. These feasts are not merely celebratory; they serve a vital purpose in the cosmological structure of Norse mythology, representing a cyclical renewal of life and death, where the heroic warrior transcends mortality and finds immortality in the service of Odin. The presence of Valkyries at these feasts transcends mere service; their participation solidifies the sacred nature of the event, emphasizing their role as guardians and custodians of the afterlife.

The narratives surrounding Valkyries also reveal aspects of their social interactions. While primarily depicted in battle or in Valhalla, glimpses into their personal lives are tantalizingly suggested. While not explicitly detailed, hints of camaraderie, competition, and even potential romantic entanglements within their ranks are implied in some sagas and poems. This hints at a complex social structure within their own ranks, beyond their roles as agents of Odin. The potential for personal relationships within this elite group of divine warriors adds layers of depth and intrigue to their cultural narrative, moving beyond their battlefield roles to reveal a more complete picture of their society.

Furthermore, the symbolism associated with Valkyries extends beyond their individual roles. They are often depicted as harbingers of fate, embodying the unpredictable and often ruthless aspects of destiny. Their presence on the battlefield isn't simply a matter of selecting the slain; it is a manifestation of the broader Norse cosmological concept of Wyrd, the inescapable force of fate that shapes the course of events. The Valkyries, therefore, become more than individual agents; they represent the active embodiment of this powerful force, weaving their choices into the tapestry of destiny. Their actions, however seemingly arbitrary, are part of a larger, cosmic plan, emphasizing their role as instruments of a higher power, inextricably linked to the very fabric of existence.

The descriptions of Valkyries' appearance further contribute to their rich cultural context. They are not merely human-like figures; their depictions often incorporate elements of the supernatural, reflecting their hybrid nature as both divine beings and agents of the mortal world. Their garments, their weaponry, even their physical attributes – such as their ability to shift shapes or their ethereal beauty – reinforce their otherworldly nature and highlight their unique position within the Norse pantheon. These attributes are not mere embellishments; they are integral to their representation, emphasizing the blurred lines between the realms and reinforcing their status as connectors between the mortal and divine spheres.

The myths and legends associated with Valkyries are not static; they evolved over time, reflecting the changing cultural values and beliefs of the Norse people. The stories, passed down through generations of oral tradition and later recorded in written sagas, provide valuable insights into their evolving cultural significance. The narratives reveal a gradual shift in their depiction, from figures primarily associated with death and battle to entities with a more nuanced and complex role within the broader cosmology. This evolution reflects the changing societal perceptions of warfare, heroism, and the afterlife, highlighting the dynamic and adaptable nature of Norse mythology.

Finally, the legacy of the Valkyries extends beyond the confines of Norse mythology. Their imagery and symbolism have resonated with artists, writers, and filmmakers for centuries, inspiring countless reinterpretations and reimaginings. From operatic portrayals to contemporary fantasy literature, the enduring appeal of Valkyries demonstrates their lasting cultural impact and their continued ability to capture the imagination. This enduring influence testifies not just to their mythological significance, but also to the inherent power of their cultural representation – a powerful blend of grace, strength, and the inevitability of fate. Their story remains a potent symbol of heroic death, divine judgment, and the enduring allure of the mysterious and the supernatural.

.

Their role in funeral rituals and the afterlife

The Valkyries, those enigmatic figures of Norse mythology, hold a pivotal and multifaceted role not merely in the chaotic battles of the gods but also in the solemn, deeply significant rituals surrounding death and the subsequent journey to the afterlife. Their involvement transcends a simple escort service; their actions shape the very nature of the transition from earthly existence to the halls of Valhalla or the chilling expanse of Hel. Far from passive observers, the Valkyries actively participate in the shaping of the afterlife, their choices determining the destiny of fallen warriors, influencing the balance of power in the cosmos, and reflecting the complex Norse understanding of death and honor.

Their influence begins even before the final breath. While the battlefield carnage provides the primary stage for their actions, the funeral rites themselves represent a crucial intersection between the mortal and the divine realms, a space where the Valkyries' agency is heavily emphasized. The meticulous preparations for a warrior's funeral, a testament to societal values and spiritual beliefs, served as an implicit invitation for the Valkyries to attend. The elaborate preparation of the body, the construction of the funeral pyre, and the poignant lamentations accompanying the cremation were not just rituals of mourning but powerful invocations, actively drawing the Valkyries' attention and influencing their choices. The grander and more elaborate the funeral, the more likely it was that the deceased would gain the Valkyries' favor and find themselves welcomed into the glorious halls of Valhalla. Conversely, a neglected burial, devoid of the appropriate rituals and fanfare, might signal a lack of worthy deeds or a life deemed less significant, resulting in a different, perhaps less desirable, afterlife destination.

The very act of choosing the slain is not random; it is deeply selective, reflecting a sophisticated judgment on the warrior's merit. The Valkyries were not merely messengers of fate but discerning judges, meticulously assessing the valor, skill, and adherence to the warrior code displayed by those who fell in battle. The selection process, though shrouded in myth and mystique, hinted at a rigorous evaluation of each warrior's life, highlighting the Norse emphasis on individual agency and the importance of a life lived with honor and courage. Their choices were not arbitrary; they reflected a divine assessment of the deceased's worthiness, a cosmic judgment that shaped the individual's journey into the afterlife. The manner in which the Valkyries selected – whether by appearing in a majestic display of power or subtly guiding a warrior's soul – underscores the profound connection between death, honor, and the divine intervention in the fate of the fallen.

The afterlife itself, as depicted in Norse mythology, is inextricably linked to the Valkyries' actions. Their role extends beyond the simple selection of souls; they actively shape the experience of the afterlife for those they choose. Those selected for Valhalla, the glorious hall of Odin, were assured a life of eternal feasting, camaraderie, and preparation for Ragnarök, the apocalyptic battle. This privilege, a reward bestowed only upon the most worthy warriors, speaks volumes about the Valkyries' importance in shaping the very fabric of the afterlife. They are not mere guides; they are actively responsible for ensuring the worthy find their place in the cosmic battle to come.

Conversely, those not deemed worthy of Valhalla might find themselves in Hel, a realm far less appealing. While the specifics of the Valkyries' role in guiding individuals to Hel remain less explored in existing mythology, their absence in the selection process implicitly signifies a negative judgment, a consequence of a life less lived according to the heroic ideal. This implication highlights the power of the Valkyries' choices not just in determining the location of the afterlife but also in emphasizing the Norse worldview of merit and reward. Their actions weren't simply an act of transporting souls; they represented a powerful affirmation of a life lived well, a life that merited a place of honor in the afterlife.

The Valkyries' impact extends beyond the individual souls they choose. Their actions contribute significantly to the broader cosmology of Norse mythology. By selecting the warriors who populate Valhalla, they directly influence the balance of power in the upcoming Ragnarök. Their choices shape the very composition of Odin's army, determining the strength and composition of the forces poised to fight against the encroaching chaos. Thus, their role extends beyond individual destinies; it encompasses the very fate of the cosmos itself, illustrating the profound interconnectedness between the mortal realm, the afterlife, and the destiny of the gods. Their selective process, therefore, becomes an act not only of judgment but of cosmic preservation, a key element in the larger framework of Norse mythology.

Their influence permeates the entirety of the funeral rituals, significantly impacting the afterlife experiences of fallen warriors and influencing the broader cosmic balance. Their choices, shaped by an intricate understanding of Norse values and ideals, are not merely acts of divine intervention but active participation in the shaping of death, honor, and the very destiny of the cosmos. They serve not only as guides to the afterlife, but as cosmic arbiters, their actions reflecting the complex and interwoven tapestry of Norse beliefs about life, death, and the eternal struggle between order and chaos. The intricate details surrounding their selection process and the impact of their decisions demonstrate the profound importance the Norse culture placed on the warrior's life and death, a life that was deemed worthy of meticulous judgment and potentially glorious reward in the halls of the afterlife.

.

Chapter 12: Valkyries and the Afterlife

Valkyries as guides and protectors of the dead

Valkyries, the winged maidens of Norse mythology, transcend the simplistic label of "guides" and "protectors of the dead. " Their role is far more nuanced, imbued with a potent blend of agency, divine selection, and the very shaping of the afterlife itself. They are not merely passive escorts to Valhalla, but active participants in the cosmic drama of battle, death, and the destiny of heroic souls. Their function is inherently selective, their choices reflecting a divine judgment that extends beyond mere mortality. The battlefield is not just a site of carnage; it is a stage upon which the Valkyries perform their critical task, discerning the worthy from the unworthy, the heroes from the fallen. Their presence on the battlefield, amidst the chaos and violence, is not merely symbolic; it is a demonstration of active participation in the very process of death, a process they control and shape. They are not simply collecting the dead; they are choosing them, bestowing the ultimate honor of entry into Odin's hall. This selection process is not arbitrary; it is a divine assessment of courage, skill, and adherence to the warrior ethos, qualities vital to the strength and prosperity of Asgard itself. The implications reach far beyond individual souls; the Valkyries' choices directly impact the composition of the Einherjar, the elite warrior force that safeguards Asgard. The strength of Odin's army, and by extension the survival of the gods, depends upon the Valkyries' discerning judgment.

This active participation extends beyond the battlefield. The Valkyries are not merely passive recipients of fallen warriors; they actively engage in the process of shaping the fate of the fallen. Their very appearance on the field, often described in vivid, awe-inspiring terms, is intended to inspire valor and to claim those deemed worthy. Their choices are not made in a void; they reflect a deep understanding of the warrior's code, a keen awareness of the individual's deeds, and a direct connection to the divine will. This is a far cry from the simple notion of guiding souls to the afterlife; their role is one of divine judgment, a selection process that determines the fate of the warrior, the composition of Odin's army, and ultimately, the destiny of the gods themselves. The imagery associated with them—their winged mounts, their gleaming armor, their lances dripping with the blood of battle—all underscore their active role in the shaping of destiny. They are not passive observers; they are powerful agents, wielding the authority to choose and to shape the very fabric of the afterlife.

The protection offered by the Valkyries goes beyond a simple escort. It represents a divine guarantee of honor and glory. The warriors chosen by the Valkyries are not merely transported to the afterlife; they are elevated to a position of unparalleled esteem. Their inclusion in the Einherjar is a testament to their valor, a recognition of their contributions to the greater cosmic struggle. This protection extends even beyond death itself; the very act of being chosen by a Valkyrie ensures a place of honor, remembrance, and continued significance within the Norse cosmology. Their protection is not simply a safeguard against oblivion but a pathway to immortality, to a place within the heart of the Norse pantheon. The narrative surrounding Valkyries subtly shifts the focus from the simple act of death to the profound consequences and implications of that death, elevating the process to one of divine judgement and cosmic significance. They are not simply guiding the dead; they are ensuring the preservation of heroic memory and its contribution to the ongoing struggle between the gods and the forces of chaos.

Beyond their battlefield roles, the narratives surrounding Valkyries reveal a deeper connection to the cyclical nature of life and death in Norse mythology. Their choices are not solely focused on the present; they reflect a wider understanding of the ongoing cosmic struggle between order and chaos. The warriors they choose are those who embody the values necessary for the survival of Asgard, those who will actively participate in the inevitable final battle of Ragnarok. Their function is therefore not merely an act of post-mortem escort but an active contribution to the future, a selection process that determines the composition of the force that will ultimately decide the fate of the cosmos. Their actions are thus inherently linked to the broader mythological context, underscoring their significance beyond the individual level. They are not merely guides but architects of the future, shaping the very composition of the forces that will determine the fate of the gods.

Furthermore, the depiction of Valkyries in various sagas and poems reveals a complexity that surpasses simple guardianship. They are depicted as possessing human-like emotions, capabilities, and even flaws. They are not devoid of agency; they actively exercise their judgment and demonstrate a capacity for both compassion and ruthless efficiency. This human-like quality adds another layer to their role, adding an element of personalization to their selection process and reinforcing the idea that their choices are not arbitrary but based on careful consideration of the individual's merits. They are agents of destiny, weaving together the threads of individual lives with the grand tapestry of the cosmic struggle, demonstrating a profound understanding of both the individual and the universal. This multifaceted portrayal prevents a reductionist view of their role to mere conductors of souls; their impact is deeply intertwined with the very nature of heroic virtue and the cosmic significance of the warrior's life and death.

The Valkyries, therefore, represent more than simple guides and protectors; they are active participants in the divine drama of life, death, and the shaping of the afterlife. Their role extends beyond simple transportation of souls; it encompasses a critical selection process, the preservation of heroic memory, and a profound influence on the very course of the cosmic struggle. Their agency, their divine judgment, and their direct impact on the composition of the Einherjar and the fate of Asgard elevate them beyond simple custodians of the dead to become powerful agents of cosmic destiny, shaping the afterlife and influencing the very fabric of Norse mythology. They are the architects of Valhalla, the arbiters of heroic valor, and the weavers of the destiny of the gods themselves. Their legacy is not simply one of guiding souls but one of shaping the very course of Norse cosmology, a profound legacy that continues to fascinate and inspire. The complexity of their roles reflects the richness and depth of Norse mythology itself, a mythology that continues to resonate with contemporary audiences due to its exploration of universal themes of life, death, and the eternal struggle between order and chaos. Their power transcends mere guardianship; it extends into the realms of divine judgment and the shaping of ultimate destinies.

.

Their influence on the realms of Valhalla and Hel

The Valkyries, those ethereal figures of Norse mythology, wield far more influence than simply selecting the slain for their respective afterlives. Their actions directly shape the very fabric of both Valhalla and Hel, the realms of Odin and Hel respectively, impacting not only the populations of these realms but their ongoing power dynamics and ultimate destinies. Their choices are not arbitrary; they reflect a nuanced understanding of the fallen warrior's merits, their potential for glory in Odin's hall, and their suitability for Hel's dominion. A Valkyrie's selection isn't merely a passive act of ferrying souls; it's an active shaping of the afterlife's composition, ensuring the continued strength and vitality (or decay, in Hel's case) of these parallel worlds. This influence extends beyond mere numerical representation; the Valkyries' choices contribute to the ongoing conflicts and alliances within both realms, determining the balance of power between warriors in Valhalla and the souls struggling under Hel's reign. The inherent qualities of those chosen – courage, loyalty, skill in battle – directly contribute to the character and strength of Odin's army, constantly bolstering its readiness for Ragnarök. Conversely, the selection of souls for Hel reflects a judgement, subtly influencing the very nature of her realm. The absence of certain types of warriors or the preponderance of others shapes the atmosphere of despair or muted defiance that permeates Hel's shadowy kingdom. The quality of the souls sent to Hel, even if reflecting punishment, also shapes the overall dynamic of her realm, impacting its power and stability relative to the vibrant and ever-growing might of Valhalla. The choices made aren't static; they reflect the ongoing battles and the ebb and flow of power in the mortal realm. As the tides of war shift, so too does the composition of Valhalla and Hel, directly reflecting the Valkyries' ongoing assessment and selection. Their agency isn't confined to the battlefield's aftermath; it extends to the very soul of the afterlife itself.

The Valkyries' influence extends beyond the mere quantitative addition of souls. The quality of those chosen heavily impacts the internal dynamics of both Valhalla and Hel. The Valkyries, acting as agents of fate, ensure that Valhalla remains a realm of formidable warriors, constantly prepared for the apocalyptic battle of Ragnarök. By selecting individuals known for their strategic prowess, unwavering loyalty, or exceptional fighting skills, they solidify Odin's army's strength and cohesion. The resulting warrior culture within Valhalla is a direct reflection of the Valkyries' discerning choices. Conversely, their selections for Hel contribute to the realm's atmosphere and its inherent challenges. The distribution of souls – those marked by treachery, cowardice, or ignominious deaths – directly affects the social strata and power dynamics within Hel's realm. This subtle, yet profound, influence shapes the daily experiences of those condemned to reside within its borders. The actions of a single Valkyrie, in selecting a particularly powerful warrior for Hel or a cunning strategist for Valhalla, can have ripple effects across both realms, altering the balance of power and potentially influencing the very outcome of future conflicts within and beyond the afterlife. This power extends beyond a simple accounting of souls; it represents a direct shaping of the destinies of these otherworldly realms.

The Valkyries' role isn't passive observation; it is active participation in the shaping of both Valhalla and Hel. They are not simply couriers of souls; they are architects of the afterlife, influencing the very essence and character of these realms through their selective choices. Their decisions are not arbitrary but rather informed judgements reflecting a complex understanding of the deceased's actions and character. The cultural and social fabric of both Valhalla and Hel is inextricably linked to the Valkyries' ongoing assessments and selections. The quality of the warriors in Valhalla, their strategic capabilities, and their collective strength, are all a direct consequence of the Valkyries' discerning choices. This isn't merely a matter of numbers; it's about shaping a formidable army for Odin, prepared for the eventual clash with the forces of chaos. Similarly, the character of Hel, its atmosphere of despair or quiet defiance, is influenced by the types of souls who populate it—a direct reflection of the Valkyries' selective process. The very power structures within these realms—the hierarchies, alliances, and tensions between their inhabitants—are subtly influenced by this selective process, making the Valkyries not merely messengers but architects of the afterlife. Their actions are not just about transportation; they are about determining the fate and character of the divine and the damned.

Moreover, the ongoing conflicts and alliances within both Valhalla and Hel are subtly, yet profoundly, influenced by the Valkyries' choices. The selection of specific individuals, based on their skills, loyalties, and past actions, directly impacts the power dynamics within these realms. The introduction of a particularly skilled warrior to Valhalla could upset existing hierarchies, leading to new alliances and rivalries. Conversely, the arrival of a notorious traitor in Hel could spark conflicts among the condemned souls. The Valkyries, therefore, are not just selectors of souls but also unwitting, or perhaps even knowing, agents of change within the afterlife, subtly manipulating the ongoing power struggles and societal structures within both realms. Their actions ripple through the afterlife, influencing relationships, generating conflicts, and ultimately shaping the cultural and political landscape of Valhalla and Hel. The narrative of these realms is not just a consequence of their inhabitants but is intricately woven with the Valkyries' choices, making their role far more significant than simply transporting souls from the battlefield to the afterlife.

The Valkyries' influence transcends mere numbers and extends to the very essence of Valhalla and Hel – their culture, social structures, and power dynamics. Their choices are not solely based on merit, but also on the potential impact of the chosen souls on the ongoing narratives within these realms. A subtle shift in selection criteria, perhaps favoring warriors known for strategic brilliance over brute strength, could profoundly alter the character of Odin's army, leading to different approaches to warfare and a changed military strategy. Similarly, the introduction of individuals with specific skills or personalities could drastically impact the social and political landscape of Hel, creating new alliances and shifting power structures amongst the condemned. Therefore, the Valkyries' influence extends beyond a simple population count and encompasses a complex interplay of factors, contributing to the ongoing evolution of these realms and their unique identities. Their actions, seemingly simple choices on a battlefield, have ramifications that ripple through eternity. The Valkyries are not passive observers; they are active participants in the ongoing saga of the afterlife, their decisions shaping the very destinies of Valhalla and Hel. Their influence is a continuous process, reflecting the dynamic nature of the mortal world and its constant impact on the realm of the dead. The ongoing battles and shifting power structures in the mortal world are mirrored and magnified within the afterlife, thanks to the continuous selections and influence of the Valkyries. Their decisions are more than simple transportations; they are the threads that weave the tapestry of the afterlife, defining the very essence of both Valhalla and Hel.

.